Living in Divine Space

Kabbalah and Meditation

Rabbi Yitzchak Ginsburgh

THE TEACHINGS OF KABBALAH SERIES

By Rabbi Yitzchak Ginsburgh
(in English)

The Hebrew Letters
Channels of Creative Consciousness

The Mystery of Marriage
How to Find True Love and Happiness in Marriage

Awakening the Spark Within
Five Dynamics of Leadership That Can Change the World

Transforming Darkness into Light
Kabbalah and Psychology

Rectifying the State of Israel
A Political Platform based on Kabbalah

Living in Divine Space
Kabbalah and Meditation

Living in Divine Space

Kabbalah and Meditation

Rabbi Yitzchak Ginsburgh

Linda Pinsky Publications
a division of Gal Einai Institute

Jerusalem

THE TEACHINGS OF KABBALAH SERIES

LIVING IN DIVINE SPACE: KABBALAH AND MEDITATION

RABBI YITZCHAK GINSBURGH

Printed in the United States of America and Israel
First Edition

Copyright © 5763 (2003) by GAL EINAI

For information:

USA: GAL EINAI
         PO Box 41
         Cedarhurst, NY 11516-9862,
         tel/fax (toll-free): (888) 453-0571

Israel: GAL EINAI
         PO Box 1015
         Kfar Chabad 72915
         tel. (in Israel): 1-700-700-966
         tel. (from abroad): 972-3-9608008

email: inner@inner.org.
Web: www.inner.org

GAL EINAI produces and publishes books, pamphlets, audiocassettes and videocassettes by Rabbi Yitzchak Ginsburgh. To receive a catalog of our products in English and/or Hebrew, please contact us at any of the above addresses, email orders@inner.org or call our orders department in Israel.

ISBN: 965-7146-064

THIS BOOK IS DEDICATED TO

OUR BELOVED
FAMILY IN ISRAEL

MAY THE ALMIGHTY BRING THE
TRUE AND COMPLETE REDEMPTION
WITH THE COMING OF MOSHIACH TO
ISRAEL AND THE ENTIRE WORLD
SPEEDILY IN OUR DAYS

BILL, EILEEN, AND PHILIP WELLS

"...נכון שיכתוב השיעורים שלומד בצורת ספר. בברכה להצלחה..."

"It would be proper to publish your classes in book form.
With blessings for success."

—*from a letter from the Lubavitcher Rebbe to the author, Elul 5741*

Table of Contents

Preface

In a public address in the summer of 1979, the Lubavitcher Rebbe, Rabbi Menachem Mendel Schneerson, discussed the need to develop a form of Jewish meditation suitable for our generation.[1]

The Rebbe pointed out that there are three general levels of meditation:

At its simplest, meditation is a technique for relaxation, which has become so essential in our contemporary, harried lifestyle.[2] In this context, meditation is simply a form of medicine, administered to cure a psychological ailment, such as stress, anxiety, or tension. To be successful, meditative techniques of this type need not involve explicit Jewish content, although, for the Jew, they must of course be free of association with any other belief system. (Meditation techniques that involve explicit or derivative forms of idolatrous practices are forbidden for non-Jews, as well.)

The next level of meditation involves focusing the mind and heart on God's presence in our lives and His Providence over everything, as expressed in the verse from Psalms, "I place God in front of me always."[3]

Finally, the deepest level of meditation involves the concentrated contemplation of the mysteries of the Torah. Since the time of the Ba'al Shem Tov, contemplating these mysteries and their pertinence to us in our daily lives has become the call of the hour. Indeed, the Messiah himself promised the Ba'al Shem Tov that his coming will be a consequence of "spreading your wellsprings—that which I have taught you and that which you have comprehended—to the furthest extreme."[4]

Inspired by the Rebbe's call, Rabbi Yitzchak Ginsburgh began developing a system of Jewish meditation based on the teachings of Kabbalah and Hassidism.[5] Over the years, he has taught this system in various venues, and now a number of his students are teaching it around the world.[6]

◆   ◆   ◆

The primary structural model of Rabbi Ginsburgh's system of Jewish meditation is based on the Talmudic teaching that the spiritual universe in which we live comprises seven "heavens" and the "earth" beneath them.[7] In accordance with the Talmud's description of each heaven's function, we may conceive of these seven heavens as levels of Divine consciousness through which we may ascend to consummate knowledge of God and union with Him, as follows:

- *Vilon* ("the Curtain")—our experience of God's continuous re-creation of all reality.
- *Rakia* ("the Firmament")—our experience of the letters of the Hebrew alphabet as channels of God's creative energy and the building blocks of reality.

- *Shechakim* ("the Millstones")—our experience of God calling us by name and giving us a mission to perform on earth.
- *Zevul* ("the Abode")—our experience of Jerusalem and the Holy Temple as they exist in the spiritual realm, ready to materialize themselves in the physical realm.
- *Ma'on* ("the Residence")—our experience of the Divine forces that act in nature, enabling us to emulate God in our lives.
- *Machon* ("the Resting Place")—our experience of God's ineffable Name *Havayah*, His omnipotence and omnipresence, reflected in every aspect of reality.
- *Aravot* ("the Heavens")—reaching the ultimate state of true selflessness (*bitul*) in the experience of God alone, making us a "Divine chariot," a vehicle of God, to fulfill His desire in creation.

The "earth," situated below the seven heavens and upon which the seven heavens rest,[8] is the foundation of this meditative ladder. The meditation presented in this book, "Living in Divine Space," corresponds to the earth, and is therefore the most basic meditation, intended to infuse us with a consciousness of God in this world as He reveals Himself to us through the means of the six constant commandments of the Torah. We must first master this meditation, becoming adept at "Living in Divine Space" before ascending to higher levels of Divine consciousness. It is the ground, the general orientation of Divine consciousness, from which we can learn to ascend. Some of the subsequent levels of Rabbi Ginsburgh's meditative system have been treated in other of his books.[9] With God's help, we plan to discuss the remaining levels in the future.

෴   ෴   ෴

In addition to its spiritual content, meditation is enhanced by a number of accompanying practices.

First and foremost of these is music. Throughout Jewish history, the yearning of the soul for God and its joy in living in His presence have found expression in melody. With the advent of Hassidism, there has been a flowering of Jewish creativity in this regard, as many masters and disciples have composed (or adapted) deep, meditative melodies to aid the practice of meditation and prayer.[10]

Breathing and movement have also always been an implicit element of Jewish meditation. Kabbalists and Hassidim do not always consciously practice specific breathing techniques, assume specific postures, or engage in specific movements. But the inner peace that comes with meditation fosters deep breathing, even as the yearning for God and the joy that accompany meditation give rise to serving God "with all my limbs."[11] In joy, one dances before God;[12] in longing to serve Him, one runs[13] to or "for" God.[14]

෴   ෴   ෴

The basic exposition of the ground-level meditation presented here, "Living in Divine Space," was circulated for a number of years among Rabbi Ginsburgh's students, and a preliminary edition was published in 1988 in *Ascent Quarterly* #14, p. 6-15.[15] This was later expanded into a 19-page booklet, *Living in Divine Space*, published by Gal Einai in 1996. The present book is a further elaboration of this meditation.

In addition to the main flow of ideas in the text, this book contains a wealth of more advanced material intended for seasoned students of Kabbalah and Hassidism. The shorter of these expositions appear together with the endnotes at the end of the book; the longer ones appear as supplementary essays after chapter eleven. Even the beginner will be enriched by perusing this material.

∽ ∽ ∽

Some notes on the conventions used in this book:

There are several Names for God used in the Bible and referred to here. Because of their holiness and spiritual power, it is forbidden to pronounce these names other than in prayer or when reciting a complete Biblical verse. Therefore, we have deliberately altered the transliteration of these Names, in accordance with the time-honored practice of how observant Jews pronounce them in non-liturgical contexts.

The unique, four-letter Name of God is known generally as the Tetragrammaton and is referred to in Jewish writings (and in this book, as well) as "the Name *Havayah*." We are forbidden to pronounce this Name altogether, and indeed, its correct pronunciation is not known nowadays. In liturgical concepts, the Name *Adni* is pronounced in its place; in non-liturgical contexts, the word *Hashem* ("the Name") is substituted. Due to its special sanctity, it has been intentionally abbreviated (or hyphenated) when a verse is written out in Hebrew. In English, it has been spelled with capitals ("GOD") in order to distinguish it from all the other Names of God.

The term "Bible" (*Tanach*) comprises the Torah (the Five Books of Moses); the Prophets (consisting of eight books: Joshua, Judges, Samuel, Kings, Isaiah, Jeremiah, Ezekiel, and the Twelve Prophets); and the Writings (consisting of eleven books: Psalms, Proverbs, Job, Ruth, the Song of Songs, Ecclesiastes, Lamentations, Esther, Daniel, Ezra-Nehemiah, and Chronicles).

In the text, the term "Torah" must be understood according to the context: in its narrowest sense, it refers to the Five Books of Moses, but more generally, it can refer to the entirety of the written and oral teachings, all of God's instructions to Israel given to enlighten humanity.

The term "Kabbalah" often is used to refer to the whole of the inner dimension of the Torah, including the teachings of Hassidism.

∽৯   ∽৯   ∽৯

We acknowledge here the invaluable editorial input of Rabbi and Mrs. Asher Crispe, Mrs. Rachel Gordon, Mr. Uri Kaploun, Mrs. Uriela Sagiv, and Rabbi Moshe Wisnefsky, as well as the technical assistance of the entire Gal Einai staff.

We are deeply grateful to the Almighty for being able to offer this work to the public. With our minds and hearts focused on God, may we speedily witness the advent of the Messiah and the true and complete Redemption.

Gal Einai
Jerusalem
18 Iyar 5763

Introduction

Introduction

בכל לבי דרשתיך.

With all my heart I seek You.[1]

Seeking God with all our hearts is the essence of Jewish meditation. The objective of Judaism in general, and that of Jewish meditation in particular, is to find God and reveal Him in this world.

God placed us on earth and concealed His presence in order to play with us a holy game of "hide and seek."[2] By consciously seeking Him, we bring Him joy, as it were, and thereby fulfill His desire in creation. Our deepest need is to reveal God in our lives and this is God's will as well.

The story is told of Rabbi Baruch of Mezhibuzh, the grandson of the Ba'al Shem Tov, that once, his children and their friends were playing hide and seek, and one of his children came running to him in tears. When he asked why he was crying, the child responded that in the middle of the game, while he was hiding, his friends lost interest in the game and left him. He waited and waited until he realized that no one was looking for him! And again the child broke down in tears.

Rabbi Baruch learned from this how God feels, as it were, when we stop the holy game of hide and seek in the

3

middle, either in despair of finding Him or because we lack sufficient interest to keep searching for Him.

But where do we find Him? Where do we even go to seek Him?

God reveals to us His ways—the roads along which He Himself walks[3]—in the Torah. The commandments of the Torah are the "ways of GOD,"[4] the "place" to go when seeking God.[5] If we wish to discover and sense God's continuous revelation to us on earth we must therefore meditate on those precepts of the Torah that are unrestricted by the barriers of time and space. For this reason, the most fundamental Jewish meditation is based on the six constant commandments of the Torah, as will be explained.

POINT, LINE, AREA

Kabbalah and Hassidism emphasize meditation as an essential technique in communication with God. With regard to meditation, as with regard to any growth process, they outline three stages of spiritual development: "point, line, area."[6]

Defined in the narrow sense, a "point" is zero-dimensional, a "line" is one-dimensional, and an "area" is two-dimensional. In human consciousness, the state of the zero-dimensional "point" is the experience of remaining static, not moving ahead, the sense of possessing zero velocity. The state of the one-dimensional "line" is the dynamic experience of motion at constant, unchanging speed (mathematically, this type of constant velocity is linear). The state of the two-dimensional "area" is the experience of acceleration, ever-increasing speed (mathematically, acceleration is represented as a quadratic expression).

Stages of Spiritual Development		
"point"	zero-dimensional	static
"line"	one-dimensional	motion at constant unchanging speed
"area"	two-dimensional	acceleration, ever-increasing speed

Defined in a broader, more profound sense, the "point" is not meant to be taken literally as zero-dimensional, nor is the "line" meant to be understood as one-dimensional, nor the "area" as two-dimensional. These three progressive stages are meant to be understood in relation to each other. The "point" is the point of departure on our spiritual journey ahead; the "line" is the consciousness of actually progressing toward our goal; the "area" is the experience of reaching the goal, possessing it and becoming possessed by it. Here, paradoxically, the ever-increasing state of acceleration comes to rest while we continue to experience the vital dynamic of motion. In other words, motion and rest paradoxically exist simultaneously in our consciousness.

Applied to meditation, the starting "point" is focusing on the objective, which is the search for God (as in "with all my heart, I seek You").

The "line" of meditation is its well-defined direction and includes the parameters of its orientation. These parameters are the six spatial directions surrounding us (*above-below, front-back, left-right*), each of which corresponds to one of the six constant commandments of the Torah meant to insure our constant awareness of God. (We will examine these commandments in detail shortly.)

The full "area" of meditative consciousness is becoming so engrossed in the depth of the meditation, on both the intellectual and emotional planes, that we transcend our own limited state of self-consciousness and undergo a metamorphosis, becoming one with the Divine truth embodied in the meditation.

Stages of Spiritual Development in Meditation			
"point"	starting point	focusing on objective	search for God
"line"	progressing toward goal	defining direction and parameters of orientation	six constant commandments
"area"	reaching goal	transcending self-consciousness; metamorphosis	oneness with Divine truth

THE SERVICE OF THE HEART

The sages refer to prayer as "the service of the heart."[7] Since the initial point of meditation is "with all my heart, I seek You," meditation may also be understood as "the service of the heart." Thus we see that there exists an intrinsic relationship between meditation and prayer.

Indeed, prayer is the culmination, the consummate expression, of meditation. The initial "point" of focus creates Divine structure; the final "point" within, prayer, reflects our inner experience when we enter the consciousness of "Living in Divine Space."[8] Prayer, as the "point" of the six directions of Divine space, converts the meditative "line" into a living, pulsating Divine "area."

As will be explained, prayer is the striving of the soul to transform the meditative state into Divine life, to metamorphose out of a state of *self*-consciousness into one of *Divine* consciousness.[9]

CHAPTER ONE

Meditation

CHAPTER ONE

Meditation

THE SOUL AND REALITY

The mind is the interface between the soul and reality.

All of us are constantly being bombarded with stimuli and sensations from the outside world, and it is our mind that processes this onrush of sensations. The mind determines which sensations are to be taken note of, then classifies and arranges them, and decides which response is appropriate to which stimulus, based on past experiences or principles.

It is the mind, then, that determines how we relate to our environment. To realize ourselves in life to the fullest extent, we must provide our mind with the proper tools to process reality and relate to it. This is a fundamental purpose of Jewish meditation.

Through meditation, we take the untamed mind and train it to think in terms of images that are based on truth. By leading a subject through deeper and deeper levels of abstraction, we reach and affect deeper and deeper dimensions of the mind, thus gradually changing ourselves and the way we respond to the world around and within us.

11

To this end, seasoned practitioners of meditation will make use of the whole range of Biblical, Talmudic, Kabbalistic, and Hassidic literature to fertilize the potent ground of their imagination and faculty of association. When evaluated in the context of Torah, knowledge of science and nature, God's creation, can also be summoned to the same end. The aim is to produce a conceptual garden of ever-evolving multi-dimensional images and insights into reality that will serve as the context and content of meditation.

METHODOLOGY

In Jewish meditation, we strive to understand in depth the Divine truths embodied in the Torah and in the marvels of God's creation (which in themselves bind us to God the Creator and to His Torah); we also strive to establish points of connection between them and our personal life.

We enhance the potency of our meditation by *hearing* the holy words of the Torah (ideally in Hebrew, the language of creation) and simultaneously *envisioning* the holy letters.[1] We consider/count the holy letters as we would count precious jewels, one by one.[2] Enamored by each letter, unable to let go and leave it in order to pass on to the next letter, we bind each letter to the next one, as one binds one flower to another, thereby creating a beautiful bouquet.[3] True love of the letters of the Torah comes from realizing that God has, so to speak, given Himself to us in them.[4]

To this end, we will anchor each concept we present in this exposition to its source in the Torah, to specific words and phrases taken from the Bible.

TO KNOW GOD

Jewish meditation begins with the awareness that God has instructed us to meditate on Him and His omnipresence, in order to experience Him (i.e., to know Him) in every facet of our lives. We first commit ourselves to fulfill His command. The Torah states:[5]

> *You shall know this day and take to heart that GOD is God in the heavens above and on the earth below, there is no other.*

In the *Tanya*,[6] the classic text of Hassidic thought, Rabbi Shneur Zalman of Liadi concurs with the opinion of those rabbinic authorities[7] who count this verse as one of the 613 commandments of the Torah, defining it as the commandment "to know God" by contemplating God and His continual creation of the universe.

In meditation, our hearts are aroused to turn away from those egocentric pursuits that normally fill our consciousness, all being illusory states of existence. Instead, we turn toward the one, true reality, God.

As is the case with regard to all human endeavors, the effectiveness of meditation is clearly a gift from God.[8] However, we are granted free choice, which we must utilize to its maximal extent. In the case of meditation, we must search for God from the depths of our hearts in order to be worthy of the gift of Divine revelation.

Additionally, in order for the seeds of meditation to take root in the soul, to grow and bear fruit, we ourselves must become fertile "earth." This depends upon our spiritual acquisition of humility and selflessness.

Many beginners mistakenly understand meditation as an attempt to clear the mind and thereby transcend the normative thought process. Clearing the mind of foreign thoughts that disturb the focus of meditation is definitely a prerequisite to entering the meditative state, but it is not the essence of meditation itself. Kabbalah and Hassidism teach that meditation involves thought, for meditation is the search to find God not only abstractly but concretely as well.

Meditation is intended to translate Divine insight, as perceived instinctively by the Divine soul, into the context of the natural, "dark" intelligence of the so-called "animal" soul, that basic aspect of the life force that animates our physical selves. We achieve this through clear and well-directed thought, making use of precise parables, metaphors, and psychological or physical examples related to the Divine concepts that compose the essence of our meditation.

For example, the Divine concept of creation *ex nihilo* ("out of nothing") might be translated into a context understood by the animal soul via the parable of the seed. By meditating on how the seed must rot in the ground, returning to a relative state of "nothing" before it sprouts into a plant, we are able to intellectually grasp the idea of God's constant re-creation of the world.

Through in-depth meditation, we refine our intellect (which in itself is a gift of God) to become a channel for Divine consciousness, allowing it to permeate our day-to-day consciousness, our normative state of being.

With all of these thoughts in mind, we will now turn to our meditation—"Living in Divine Space."

CHAPTER TWO

The Six Constant Commandments

The Six Constant Commandments

THE DUTIES OF THE HEART

The meditation presented here is a truly basic one in Jewish spiritual life.[1] It embodies many of the fundamental teachings of Judaism, and moreover can serve as a filter through which we may process virtually all aspects of reality. As such, it is a prime example of the purpose of Jewish meditation as explained earlier.

We will center our meditation on the six constant commandments of the 613 commandments of the Torah.[2]

Implicitly, on the spiritual plane, all of the commandments of the Torah apply to each and every Jew at all times and in all places, as taught by the Ba'al Shem Tov, the 18th century founder of the Hassidic movement. Explicitly, however, on the physical plane,[3] only six of the 613 apply to all Jews at all times and in all places, inasmuch as they are "duties of the heart."[4] These are:

- to believe in the existence and providence of God,
- not to believe that any other gods exist,
- to believe that God is One—an absolute, non-composite, and all-encompassing unity,
- to love God,

- to fear God, i.e., to be in awe of Him, and
- to shield one's mind from negative thoughts.

These six commandments are enumerated in the introduction to *Sefer HaChinuch*,[5] which refers to them allegorically as "the six cities of refuge." The cities of refuge were six cities designated by the Torah[6] to serve as refuge for those guilty of manslaughter. This unintentional act of manslaughter was brought about by a faulty state of consciousness. The guilty individual was instructed to flee to one of the six cities. He was to remain within the city of refuge until his sin was atoned for, by the death of the High Priest. (Indeed, even upon leaving the physical city, he never leaves the rectified state of consciousness that he acquired there. He takes the "space" of the refuge city with him for the rest of his life.)

Similarly, every Jew is instructed to correct his or her state of consciousness by entering *all* of the six constant commandments of the Torah, thereby abiding within the spiritual "space" they create and remaining continuously conscious of God's presence.[7]

CONSTRUCTING A SPIRITUAL SANCTUARY

Essentially, the meditation of "Living in Divine Space" involves constructing a spiritual sanctuary around oneself, a cube[8] defined by the six constant commandments, as follows:

- *above*: belief in the existence and providence of God
- *below*: negation of belief in other gods
- *front*: belief that God is one
- *right*: love of God
- *left*: fear of God
- *back*: shielding the mind from negative thoughts

In the quintessential statement of Judaism, the *Shema*, "Hear O Israel, GOD is our God, GOD is one,"[9] the sages perceive the Hebrew word for "one," *echad*, as alluding to the six directions of space. *Echad* is spelled *alef, chet, dalet;* the numerical values of these letters are 1, 8, and 4, alluding to God being one (1) in all seven heavens and earth (8) and four lateral directions (4).[10] In our spiritual sanctuary, *above* corresponds to the seven heavens, *below* to the earth, and the four lateral directions—east, west, south, and north—to *front, back, right,* and *left,* respectively. (The Torah's directional orientation faces east/sunrise; thus, south is to the *right,* north to the *left,* and west/sunset behind.)

In Hassidism, we are taught that human consciousness develops from first recognizing the vertical space coordinate of *above-below,* and only thereafter, incorporating into our spatial consciousness the horizontal and lateral coordinates of *front-back* and *right-left.* This is the order of the letters of *echad,* as well as the order of the meditation on the six constant commandments of the Torah (as will be explained).

above	believe in the existence of God
below	do not believe in any other gods
front/east	believe that God is one
right/south	love God
left/north	fear God
back/west	shield the mind from negative thoughts

EMOTIONS OF THE HEART

In Kabbalah, the six sides of the cube correspond to the six emotions of the heart that originate in the supernal *sefirot*, the channels of Divine light and energy with which God creates the world. In particular, the six *sefirot* that correspond to the six emotions of the heart correspond, as well, to the six days of creation.

Each of these channels/emotions of the heart also possesses an inner "light" or soul-experience as follows:

The *sefirah* of *chesed* ("loving-kindness") possesses the inner light of *ahavah* ("love"). On the first day of creation God created light with love.

The *sefirah* of *gevurah* ("might") possesses the inner light of *yirah* ("fear"). On the second day of creation God separated the higher waters from the lower waters by creating the firmament with fear.

The *sefirah* of *tiferet* ("beauty") possesses the inner light of *rachamim* ("mercy"). On the third day God created life on earth, including vegetation and beautiful, fruit-bearing trees, with mercy.

The *sefirah* of *netzach* ("victory" and "eternity") possesses the inner light of *bitachon* ("trust"). On the fourth day, God created the sun and the moon, the two great luminaries, which symbolize the transcendent light and the immanent light of God (which we cannot directly see, but the presence of which we sense and become inspired by when we trust in God).

The *sefirah* of *hod* ("thanksgiving" or "splendor") possesses the inner light of *temimut* ("sincerity" or "simplicity"). On the fifth day God created the fish and the birds, the splendor of the seas and the sky, and blessed them to be fruitful and multiply (an act performed in the animal kingdom instinctively, epitomizing the attribute of simplicity).

The *sefirah* of *yesod* ("foundation") possesses the inner light of *emet* ("truth"; *yesod* validates all of the previous emotions by bringing them to consummation or fulfillment in reality). On the sixth day God created the first human being who symbolizes God's "seal of truth."

The arrangement of the six emotions of the heart and their inner lights along the sides of the cube is as follows:

emotion		inner light	day of week	direction
chesed	loving-kindness	love	Sunday	*right*/south
gevurah	might	fear	Monday	*left*/north
tiferet	beauty	mercy	Tuesday	*front*/east
netzach	victory	trust	Wednesday	*above*
hod	thanksgiving	sincerity	Thursday	*below*
yesod	foundation	truth	Friday	*back*/west

The six emotions of the heart also correspond to the six archetypal souls of the Jewish people: Abraham, Isaac, Jacob, Moses, Aaron, and Joseph.

A clear allusion to our present meditation is found in the rabbinic teaching that Adam (the soul-root of Joseph[11]) built—on the spiritual plane—the western wall of the Temple, Abraham the southern wall, Isaac the northern wall, Jacob the eastern wall, and Moses the roof. Aaron walked barefoot on the floor of the Temple. These archetypal souls and directions correspond exactly to the elements of our meditation, as we will describe it.

We will see that within the meditative cube—our spiritual sanctuary or Temple—we unite (i.e., identify ourselves) with our prayer, as King David said in Psalms, "I am prayer."[12] The commandment of prayer corresponds to the *sefirah* of *malchut* ("kingdom"), whose inner light or soul-experience is *shiflut* ("lowliness") and which corresponds to the archetypal soul of King David and to the seventh day of creation, Shabbat.[13]

emotion		direction	day of week	archetypal soul
chesed	loving-kindness	*right*/south	Sunday	Abraham
gevurah	might	*left*/north	Monday	Isaac
tiferet	beauty	*front*/east	Tuesday	Jacob
netzach	victory	*above*	Wednesday	Moses
hod	thanksgiving	*below*	Thursday	Aaron
yesod	foundation	*back*/west	Friday	Adam/Joseph
malchut	kingdom	sanctuary	Shabbat	David

PARTS OF THE BODY

In the course of our meditation, we must also be aware how the spatial parameters of the meditation cube correspond in Kabbalah to parts of the body. *Chesed* and *gevurah, right* and *left,* correspond to the right arm and left arm. *Netzach* and *hod, above* and *below,* correspond to the right leg and left leg.[14] *Tiferet* and *yesod, front* and *back,* correspond to the torso and (its extension) the procreative organ.[15] *Malchut,* the midpoint of space, the inner sanctum from which we engage in prayer, corresponds to the mouth.[16]

direction	emotion		part of body
above	*netzach*	victory	right leg
below	*hod*	thanksgiving	left leg
front/east	*tiferet*	beauty	torso
right/south	*chesed*	loving-kindness	right arm
left/north	*gevurah*	might	left arm
back/west	*yesod*	foundation	procreative organ
sanctuary	*malchut*	kingdom	mouth

We will now explain in detail each of the six constant commandments in relation to our meditation cube. In doing so, we will quote the text of each commandment as it is stated in the Torah. The words of the Torah will serve as the anchor of our consciousness, the focal point of our comprehension.[17]

CHAPTER THREE

Belief

אָנֹכִי ה׳ אֱלֹהֶיךָ אֲשֶׁר הוֹצֵאתִיךָ
מֵאֶרֶץ מִצְרַיִם מִבֵּית עֲבָדִים

*I am GOD, your God, Who has taken you out of
the land of Egypt, out of the house of bondage*

—Exodus 20:2

CHAPTER THREE

Belief

Above is the commandment:

אנכי ה' אלהיך אשר הוצאתיך
מארץ מצרים מבית עבדים.

*I am GOD, your God, Who has taken you out of the
land of Egypt, out of the house of bondage.*[1]

This commandment, the first of the Ten
Commandments and also the first of the six constant
commandments of the Torah, is the mandate to believe in
God.

THE ELEMENTS OF BELIEF

Belief in God entails:

- belief in God's existence, that there is a God,
- belief that God is all powerful, and
- belief that God, in His Providence over all, redeems the soul, each and every soul, from spiritual bondage.

The first three words of the first of the Ten Commandments are *Anochi HaShem Elokecha,* which mean "I am GOD your God." In Kabbalah, they signify three aspects of Divinity:

- God's essence ("I am"),
- God's transcendent light, the light beyond our world (GOD), and
- God's immanent light, the light within our world ("your God").[2]

Clearly, these three aspects of Divinity correspond to the three elements of belief stated above:

- A Jew believes in God's very essence, of which God said, "I am whom I am."[3]
- God's transcendent light is referred to as the light that "surrounds all worlds." Surrounding reality implies the power to control it.[4]
- The belief that God, in His providence over all, redeems the soul from bondage corresponds to His immanent light, the light that "fills all worlds."

God's immanent light is His Divine Providence over all. In order for God to take us out of Egypt (a place deemed to be inescapable by natural means), His immanent light, His Providence over us, must unite with His transcendent light, which, being beyond this world, can overturn nature. This union is ultimately effected by the power of God's very essence. All three levels of Divinity thus bind together to make redemption possible: "I am GOD, your God, Who has taken you out of the land of Egypt, out of the house of bondage." (We will see presently how this relates to us today.)

Often, in Kabbalah and Hassidic teachings, God's two manifestations, His transcendent light and His immanent light, are symbolized as the "sun" and the "moon." These were created on the fourth day, the day that corresponds to the *sefirah* of *netzach* ("victory") and the direction of *above*, the direction of the first of the six constant commandments. Obviously (and as noted earlier), the creation of the heavenly bodies on the fourth day relates to the direction of *above*.

Together with the moon were created the stars, which symbolize the souls of Israel.[5] God's immanence (the "moon") relates to each and every individual soul (each and every "star").

THE OBLIGATIONS OF THE TORAH

Let us now examine the specific terminology of this commandment. The Hebrew word for "Egypt" (*Mitzraim*) also means "confinements/straits" (*metzarim*). For this reason, all states of physical and spiritual "exile" are referred to in the Torah as "Egypt." By the power of this commandment, which, as noted above is the first of the Ten Commandments, we are released from exile. Only then can we perform all of God's commandments; only when we are not slaves to any other master can we become fully-committed servants of God.[6]

We are taught[7] that "whoever accepts upon himself the obligations of the Torah is released from the obligations of the government and the obligations of earning a living. And whoever disregards the obligations of the Torah is burdened with the obligations of the government and the obligations of earning a living."

True belief in God, the Giver of the Torah, motivates us to accept upon ourselves all the obligations of the Torah, and so to experience our personal exodus from Egypt (the release/redemption from all foreign obligations). The word for "obligation" or "yoke" in Hebrew (*ol*) is spelled exactly the same (though pronounced differently) as the word for "above" (*al*), thus alluding to the state of consciousness of this commandment, the sense of the Divine *above*.

INFINITE TRUST

The emotional feeling of this commandment is one of infinite trust (*bitachon*) in God. As noted earlier, trust is the inner experience of the power of *netzach*, corresponding to the soul of Moses, through whom God gave the Torah to Israel.

Of Moses it is said, "He was the first redeemer and he shall be the final redeemer."[8] In Hassidism, we are taught that the first redemption from the physical land of Egypt was primarily the redemption from physical slavery. The final redemption, on the other hand, will be primarily the redemption from the spiritual "Egypt," the redemption from spiritual exile and confinements.

Even observant Jews, who in general walk in the ways of the Torah, can be in a state of spiritual exile.[9] The inner sparks of their souls may still be imprisoned, unable to reveal and express themselves. Moses, as the Messiah, the final redeemer, is destined to take *all* souls out of *all* states of exile. He will come to reveal in the soul of every Jew the ultimate truth about God, which is encapsulated in the words, "I am GOD, your [personal] God."

TWO STATES OF REDEMPTION

The terminology of this commandment initially appears redundant; "out of the land of Egypt" and "out of the house of bondage" seems to refer to the same place. However, there is a difference:

Redemption "out of the land of Egypt" implies freedom to express our own, independent will, our power of free choice, the prerequisite to the performance of all of the commandments of the Torah. The redemption "out of the house of bondage" implies that, ultimately, we are subordinate to no power and to no one other than God.

Although the Torah instructs us to appoint a king to rule over Israel, it emphasizes that this can only be achieved after we first unequivocally accept upon ourselves the obligations of the kingdom of God.[10] Only then may we establish an earthly kingdom ruled by a king truly devoted to manifesting God's kingdom on earth.[11]

Thus, we are essentially not subordinate to any king, neither of Israel nor of any other nation, other than to God alone.[12] Only as an extension, in devotion and commitment to God's will as expressed in the Torah, may we appoint a human king and government to rule us, but then only as long as the ruling power does not act in opposition to the obligations of the Torah.

THE WORLD TO COME

The Divine consciousness of *above* means that we never feel confined or trapped by our present state of being. To sense *above* is to sense *netzach*, to sense the World to Come, of which it is said: "'They shall go from strength to strength'—the righteous have no rest neither in this world nor in the World to Come."[13] The state of "no rest" of the World to Come is absolutely positive, itself an infinite source of pleasure. The soul is never static; it continuously rises from level to level of Divine consciousness, drawing ever closer and closer to God, the source of all good and pleasure.

In this world, to continuously rise toward God means to ever progress in our emulation of God's attributes: "just as He is merciful, so shall you be merciful."[14] Through belief in God, we can at any time break through our natural confines and rise to live at a higher, Divine level of reality.

Belief in God is the rope we use to climb upward, to connect to our soul-root, to manifest our essential potential as "an actual part of God *above*."[15]

CHAPTER FOUR

No Other

לֹא יִהְיֶה לְךָ אֱלֹהִים אֲחֵרִים עַל פָּנָי

You shall have no other gods before Me

—Exodus 20:3

CHAPTER FOUR

No Other

Below is the commandment:

לֹא יִהְיֶה לְךָ אֱלֹהִים אֲחֵרִים עַל פָּנַי.

You shall have no other gods before Me.[1]

This commandment, the second of the Ten Commandments and also the second of the six constant commandments, clearly complements the previous one.[2]

IDOLATRY

The second commandment states that we must not place our trust in "other gods."

This prohibition includes believing that anything, other than the one God, is ultimately responsible for what happens in the world.[3] If, for example, we do not recognize and acknowledge God as being the ultimate source of our livelihood, but imagine that we receive our livelihood solely from the hands and good graces of others (thus making ourselves psychologically dependent upon them), this is a subtle form of "worshipping idols."[4] Likewise, if we attribute our achievements and accomplishments in life solely to our own talents and prowess, this is a subtle form of self-worship.

Moreover, this commandment implies that we should not imagine that there is ultimate reality in what we experience as worldly causation. True, God created nature with its laws and cause-and-effect dynamics, but He controls these forces "like the axe in the hand of the woodchopper."[5] We must therefore neither look to the forces of nature or to any created being for what we want, nor feel gratitude toward them for what we have.

(With regard to other people, we may and should feel and express our gratitude for the good that they bestow us, for human souls possess free will and choose whether to give or not. This is especially the case with regard to our parents—as stated in the fifth of the Ten Commandments: "Honor your father and your mother"—who act as "partners"[6] with God in creating and caring for us.[7])

This commandment is placed *below*, for a rectified *below* means that only God is beneath us, only He supports us, and ultimately, we have no one to rely upon besides Him. All natural (or seemingly supernatural) "earthly" forces[8] are unworthy of our trust.

Continuing the imagery of the previous commandment, in which we compared the belief in God alone to a rope we use to climb upward to connect to our soul-root, we can say that as soon as (and to the extent that) we disconnect from this rope, we start to fall into the quicksand of reliance on natural forces.[9]

THE PATH OF LIFE

By constantly eliminating any mixed loyalties or foreign allegiances, we become whole and complete in our sincere commitment to God alone.[10] Sincerity (*temimut*) is the inner experience of the Divine power of *hod* ("thanksgiving"), corresponding to the soul of Aaron, as noted earlier.

Throughout the Bible, the attribute of sincerity is linked idiomatically to the verb "to walk" (as in, "he who walks sincerely..."[11]), or to the noun "way/path" (as in, "happy are those of the sincere path..."[12]).

We walk the path of life on earth below. In Kabbalah, "walking" is associated in particular with the left leg ("the left leg controls the sense of walking"[13]), corresponding to the Divine power of *hod*, the spatial parameter of *below*.

As we have seen, the first of the six constant commandments entails a consciousness of "going/walking from strength to strength," *above*, in the eternal state of the World to Come. Its complement, the second commandment, entails a consciousness of "walking from strength to strength," below, in this world. Both of them entail a gradual process that progresses through time. Together with this sense of time comes a consciousness of the *above-below* coordinate of space.

CHAPTER FIVE

Unity

שמע ישראל ה׳ אלהינו ה׳ אחד

Hear O Israel, GOD is our God, GOD is one

—Deuteronomy 6:4

CHAPTER FIVE

Unity

To the *front* is the commandment:

שמע ישראל ה' אלהינו ה' אחד.

Hear O Israel, GOD is our God, GOD is one.[1]

This statement, known as the *Shema*, is our quintessential affirmation of the unity of God and also the third constant commandment. It mandates us "to hear"[2] God's absolute oneness in the inner ear of our soul and to contemplate His perfect unity. Although, in this world, we cannot see with our physical eyes God's absolute unity in creation—for which reason we cover our eyes when proclaiming "Hear, O Israel…"—we can "hear" or "understand" it in our hearts.

ALL IS ONE

Here, we begin our meditation by recalling that all experiences impinging on our consciousness originate ultimately from one single source, namely God, and then we further contemplate the truth that God, whose essence encompasses all being, is the only ultimate reality.

43

In our contemplation of the second commandment, we negated all forms of idolatry, realizing that worldly causation possesses no ultimate reality. Now we come to the deeper realization that in truth God is the only ultimate reality—"there is no other besides Him."[3]

The logical order of the first three of the six constant commandments is thus, that first we believe in the existence of God, then we negate all other gods, and then we come to the full recognition of God's absolute existence as the one and only true existence.

FAITH IN PARTICULAR

Whereas the first of the Ten Commandments is referred to in Kabbalah and Hassidism as "faith in general," this commandment, to unify God in faith, is referred to as "faith in particular."[4] While "faith in general" is *above* us, "faith in particular" is in *front* of us.

"Faith in general" implies the experience of God being with us and looking over us from *above*[5] at all times. All takes place within the context of Divine Providence. God's transcendence is not removed from reality, but oversees reality.

"Faith in particular" implies the recognition of God's absolute unity in all facets of reality as they present themselves in the forefront of our consciousness from moment to moment.[6] Not only does God oversee reality, but He is the very essence of all reality.

ALL IS GOOD

The implications of this fundamental tenet of our faith in God's absolute unity are wide-ranging and profound. For if everything we experience comes from (and ultimately *is*) God, who is obviously the ultimate good,[7] then everything must be ultimately good. The fact that something appears to be bad (and, when met out by humans, is indeed a punishable wrong) is only due to the limited scope of our vision of what has transpired, its immediate and long term ramifications, distorted, as well, by our own idea of how things should be.

The sages say that "when one gets angry, it is as if he is serving idols."[8] This is a powerful (one could even say extreme) statement. But upon reflection, what really causes anger? When things don't go *my* way, I get angry; the world is not conforming to *my* vision of perfection. But since God is ultimately in control, this is tantamount to saying that I consider my version of the world better than His! This is a subtle form of idol worship: I am enthroning my intellect and ego and paying homage to them.

(Of course, when humans are to blame for the wrongs of the world, it is at times necessary to show anger, in care for them and for the world, and in order to rectify the wrongs they have caused and to influence them to change their ways. However, when this can be accomplished "in ways of pleasantness,"[9] without even appearing to get angry, such an approach is preferable.)

Now, of course, not everyone who gets angry consciously realizes this, but the point is that constant awareness of the unity of God is the surest antidote for anger, as well as a host of other psychological maladies we would all do better without.

Hence, the importance of keeping this awareness "in *front*" of us at all times.[10]

GOD'S MERCY

As the sages teach, the Name *Havayah* signifies God's attribute of mercy whereas the Name *Elokim* signifies His attribute of judgment.[11] Accordingly, this commandment can be interpreted: "Hear, O Israel: GOD [*Havayah*, the all-merciful] is our God [*Elokim*, who appears to us in nature through His attribute of judgment, yet] GOD [*Havayah*] is one [all is but an aspect of His absolute mercy]."[12]

The ability to view all the seemingly divergent phenomena of life as manifestations of one, absolutely merciful source, is unique to the Jewish people. For this reason, in the verse "Hear, O Israel...," the name *Israel* stands out. As opposed to any other generic name of the Jewish people, "Israel" signifies the experience of the Jewish soul in its absolute, pure state, as "an actual part of God above."[13]

This is also why this verse is the central statement of Judaism. Not only does our faith in God's absolute unity come here to the fore, but the essence of our own soul-root—Israel—comes to the fore as well.

In the book of Isaiah, Israel is symbolized as a tree.[14] Every Jewish soul corresponds to a letter of the Torah, "the Tree of Life." Life in general appears for the first time on the third day of creation, the day that corresponds to the *sefirah* of *tiferet* ("beauty") and the direction of *front*. In the Torah, the Hebrew root of *tiferet* is used to describe the beautiful foliage of a tree,[15] the apex of the creation of the third day. Furthermore, the Messiah himself, the greatest of all souls of Israel, is referred to as a "plant" by the prophets.[16]

When we internalize the commandment to "Hear, O Israel, GOD is our God, GOD is one," we partake of the Tree of Life and rectify the primordial sin of eating the forbidden fruit of the other tree, the Tree of Knowledge of Good and Evil.

"Hear, O Israel..." is the understanding and knowledge that the ultimate origin of what appears to us to be good or what appears to us to be bad is all Divine goodness and mercy. This knowledge we place in the *front* of our consciousness always.

To Emulate the Creator

Through the commandment to know God we become aware of our own Divine inner nature, and inspire to live up to it, that is, to emulate our Creator. Because mercy (*rachamim*) is God's most essential attribute (for mercy implies empathy, and thus, more than any other of His attributes, reflects God's oneness with His creation), meditation on the unity of God produces feelings of mercy within the soul.

These feelings of mercy are directed firstly to the Godly sparks within other people[17] and then to all of reality at large. We redeem the Godly sparks from their spiritual exile by spreading the awareness/consciousness of one, good and merciful God. [18]

CHAPTER SIX

Love

ואהבת את ה׳ אלהיך בכל לבבך
ובכל נפשך ובכל מאדך

And you shall love GOD your God with all your heart,
and with all your soul, and with all your might

—Deuteronomy 6:5

CHAPTER SIX

Love

To the *right* is the commandment:

ואהבת את ה' אלהיך בכל לבבך
ובכל נפשך ובכל מאדך.

*And you shall love GOD your God with all your heart,
and with all your soul, and with all your might.*[1]

This commandment directly follows the verse of the *Shema* in the Torah. It is also the fourth constant commandment, which mandates us to love God. Love of God is the emotion that motivates the fulfillment of all the 248 positive commandments of the Torah.[2]

ONENESS AND LOVE

In the Torah, this commandment follows the previous one ("Hear, O Israel..."), indicating that loving God is the natural result of contemplating His unity.[3]

But it seems odd that we should be "commanded" to love something or someone. Generally, we associate "commandments" with *action* (or, as in the case of the constant commandments discussed earlier, with focused

51

thought, a process under the control of the mind) rather than with *emotion* (which in general is not under the control of the mind; one cannot simply choose in one's mind to love and then experience the emotion of love).

Indeed, the Ba'al Shem Tov teaches that this commandment is not an injunction for us to directly activate the emotion of love; rather, it mandates us to first contemplate the unity and greatness of God, a contemplation that is intended to *spontaneously* arouse love for Him.[4] For if God is in fact the ultimate source of all reality, who could desire to love anything other than Him? And conversely, if everything else we perceive indeed possesses no intrinsic reality, why bother devoting our energy to it?[5]

LOVE LIKE WATER AND FIRE

This commandment is placed to the *right* in our meditation cube, since, in Jewish imagery, the right side is associated with the emotion of love and the attribute of loving-kindness.[6] As noted earlier, *right* corresponds to the south, which symbolizes a feeling of warmth toward God and Israel. The Ba'al Shem Tov would place his right hand over the heart of a Jewish boy and bless him to be "a warm Jew."

In Hassidic teachings, the experience of warmth is called "love like fire." Indeed, the numerical value of the entire phrase "with all your heart, and with all your soul, and with all your might" is identical with that of the Hebrew word for "flame" (*shalhevet*, 737). The sages allude to the ever-ascending love for God as "a fully ignited flame."[7] One

ignites the flame of love by meditating on the unity of God—
"GOD is one."

In Hassidism, we are taught that without meditation,
we may manifest "love like water," but only by the deep and
sincere meditation of the heart, searching for God with our
entire being, do we bear in our soul "love like fire."[8] "Love
like water" is like the love of brother and sister; "love like
fire" is like the love of husband and wife.

God created light, the source of warmth, on the first
day of creation, the day that corresponds to the *sefirah* of
chesed ("loving-kindness") and the direction of *right*. We are
taught that God hid the original light, for this light is indeed
the Divine creative power of love with which God created all
of reality. Would God's infinite love for every one of His
creations be revealed, no being could exist as an independent
entity. This would negate God's ultimate purpose in creation,
that He dwell in the lower realms, in a world that possesses
an independent sense of self.

Nonetheless, in every generation, the good and the
just reveal a portion of the hidden light by loving God and
Israel and by lovingly studying and teaching God's Torah, His
blueprint of creation. With the coming of the Messiah, and
subsequently in the World to Come, when there will no
longer be any need for the free choice of self-conscious
entities, God's infinite love for all will become fully revealed.

The equivalence of the original light of creation with
God's love for creation is reflected in the fact that the very
word for "love" in Hebrew, *ahavah*, is an acronym for *Or
HaKadosh Baruch Hu*, meaning "the light of the Holy One,
blessed be He."

THREE LEVELS OF LOVE

In particular, this commandment speaks of the three ascending levels of love for God: "with all your heart, and with all your soul, and with all your might." The sages[9] teach us that in the phrase "with all your heart," the word for "your heart" (*levavcha*) is spelled with a double *beit*, implying that we are to love God "with both your inclinations, with the good inclination and the evil inclination." "With all your soul" means "even if He takes your soul." And "with all your might" means that "with every measure that He measures to you, thank Him exceedingly."

In accordance with our meditation, we may see reflected in these three ascending levels of love the three previous constant commandments of the Torah:

The redemption from Egypt, from the house of bondage, is the redemption from being enslaved by our evil inclination. When freed from slavery (that is, from the evil side of our personality), we are able to elevate it, to employ it in our service of God. This is the meaning of loving God with our whole heart, with both of our inclinations, good and (elevated) evil. It is indeed the evil inclination (the source of all passion) that, when elevated, ignites the spark of love, transforming "love as water" (the innate love of the good inclination) into "love as fire."

To totally renounce idolatry, not to bow down to an idol even at the cost of one's life, is the explicit meaning of loving God "with all your soul"—"even if He takes your soul."

To thank God for every measure He measures out to us in life is to recognize His absolute oneness, His infinite mercy over all. Whether experienced as good or bad, all derives from God's goodness and mercy, which if not revealed to us now, will become revealed in the future.[10]

CHAPTER SEVEN

Fear

וְעַתָּה יִשְׂרָאֵל מָה ה׳ אֱלֹהֶיךָ שֹׁאֵל מֵעִמָּךְ
כִּי אִם לְיִרְאָה...

*And now, O Israel, what does GOD your God
ask of you, but to fear...*

—Deuteronomy 10:12

CHAPTER SEVEN

Fear

To the *left* is the commandment:

ועתה ישראל מה ה' אלהיך שאל מעמך
כי אם ליראה...

*And now, O Israel, what does GOD, your God,
ask of you, but to fear....*[1]

This, the fifth of the six constant commandments, is
the mandate to fear God, or to constantly stand in awe of
Him.[2] Fear of God is the emotion that motivates the
fulfillment of all the 365 prohibitive commandments of the
Torah.[3]

THE FEAR THAT AUGMENTS LOVE

Fear of God does not refer to the fear of punishment.
Although useful to fall back on as a means of keeping
ourselves from transgressing against God's commandments
(in times of spiritual immaturity, when unable to arouse any
deeper motivation[4]), fear of punishment is not really
considered serving God. For if we fulfill God's

commandments in order to avoid punishment, we are not fulfilling them for God's sake, but rather for our own interest.

True fear of God is founded on the fear of severing our bond of love with Him, our covenant of betrothal to Him. Thus, fear of God flows naturally out of the previous commandment, to love Him. If we truly love God, we will fear doing anything that might separate us from Him. This fear keeps our consciousness focused on God and prevents us from doing anything prohibited by the Torah.

At first, this fear is not even conscious; it is merely a natural component of our love for God.[5] Eventually, however, after we have integrated the love of God into our daily life, we may begin to sense the initial passion waning, and this is when our fear of losing our emotional connection to God surfaces. Since we recognize that our love of God is a product of our awareness of His unity, this fear inspires us to seek newer insights in our understanding of God.

Fear thus allows us to transcend the limitations of our finite consciousness.[6] Our fear of God thus joins in the process described earlier of transmuting "love as water" (natural, pleasurable love) into "love as fire" (unconsummated passion).[7] As we ascend from level to level, each level of newfound love in time becomes "second nature" to us, and again the fear of lapsing into the rut of complacency spurs us on to seek higher levels of insight with which to fan the flame of love. Thus, fear works together with love, the two joining to become the two "wings" of the soul that constantly elevate all of our good deeds, prayers, and studies.[8]

The day corresponding to the *sefirah* of *gevurah* ("might"), the consciousness of the *left*, is the second day of creation, on which God severed the lower waters from the higher waters by means of the firmament. For the first time, created reality experienced existential distance from God, the Creator. The sages teach that to this day "the lower waters cry: 'we, too, want to be close to God [as are the higher waters].'"[9] Fearing separation and longing to be close to God, creation cries out with all its might (*gevurah*) to its Creator.

THE FEAR THAT REGULATES LOVE

Just as fear serves to augment the intensity and passion of the flame of love, so does it serve to regulate our love for God. Implied in the fear of God is the apprehension of approaching Him too closely, lest the soul be annihilated in the Divine ecstasy of its passionate love for Him. This would negate God's will, for He created every being with a unique purpose in life, which cannot be fulfilled by any other being. Submission to God's will thus means restraining our passion to the extent necessary in order to remain alive and continue to fulfill our life's mission.

Here, fear creates spiritual equilibrium, *left* (fear) balancing *right* (love). This level of fear, more in alignment with God's ultimate will for creation than the previously described level of fear, is higher than the first in the root of the soul. The first level of fear is our fear of being separated from God. The second level of fear reflects God's own "fear" that the soul misinterpret its purpose.

We will presently describe an even higher, third level of fear, the essence of standing in awe in the presence of

God. Here, one no longer experiences a distinction between fear of God and loving Him.

THREE LEVELS OF FEAR

Just as the flame of love exists at three levels of ascent to God—"with all your heart, and with all your soul, and with all your might"—so does its companion, fear, exist at three levels:

The fear that our bond of love with God be severed corresponds to loving God "with all your heart." When, through the fear of God, we recognize the presence of our inner potential to sever our relationship with God—that is, our evil inclination—we elevate this very potential to serve God. In the terminology of the sages, this level of fear is called "the fear of sin" (*yirat chet*)

The fear to approach God too closely, lest one become annihilated in Divine ecstasy, corresponds to loving God "'with all your soul'—even if He takes your soul." Though we are always ready to sacrifice our life for God, we must know and take to heart that (with the few exceptions of which are said, "be killed rather than transgress"[10]) God's will is that we remain alive on earth to serve Him (even if, at times, in order to remain alive, it is necessary to transgress a precept of the Torah). The very readiness to sacrifice our life for God's sake brings us to this level of fear, which is called "the fear of God's greatness" (*yirat haromemut*). In direct proportion to the experience of "God's greatness," we must experience "human lowliness," the recognition that "God is in heaven" and "I am on earth," to live here and perform His will.[11]

In contrast to the first level of fear, "the fear of sin," this level of "the fear of God's greatness" implies standing in awe of Him. However, the ultimate state of awe in the presence of God is that of the next, highest level of fear, "shamefaced fear" (*yirat boshet*).

"Shamefaced fear" is the experience of standing in the presence of the Infinite One, feeling that He is all and all is He, and asking, "Who am I?" This corresponds to the level of "with all your might," for here, as all is God, all is a manifestation of perfect, absolute Divine goodness and mercy. In existential bashfulness, we thank Him exceedingly for every measure of life. Here, the *sefirah* of *gevurah*, whose inner experience is fear, reaches its essence, as *gevurah* means "might" (which at once implies mighty fear together with mighty love).

In general, "fear" implies "sensitivity." In Kabbalah, the left creates boundaries—that is, we identify the other and separate ourselves from the other in order to objectively sense the other's independent existence. A rectified left continues to nullify the ego and self-centeredness, for of all the emotions of the heart, fear most humbles the ego.[12] Thereafter, it is the left itself that totally overcomes separateness, in its continuous experience of God's omnipresence and omnipotence.

CHAPTER EIGHT

Loyalty

...וְלֹא תָתוּרוּ אַחֲרֵי לְבַבְכֶם וְאַחֲרֵי עֵינֵיכֶם

*And you shall not stray after your heart
and after your eyes...*

—Numbers 15:39

CHAPTER EIGHT

Loyalty

At the *back* is the commandment:

ולא תתורו אחרי לבבכם ואחרי עיניכם...

*And you shall not stray after your heart
and after your eyes....*[1]

This commandment appears in the third and concluding paragraph of the *Shema* in our daily prayers. It is the sixth and last of the six constant commandments, the mandate to guard our minds from foreign (that is, arrogant or licentious[2]) thoughts and desires. Such thoughts and desires have the negative effect of diverting our attention from God and confusing our priorities.[3] If we fulfill the first five commandments as we have described them, we will naturally want to strive to protect our precious relationship with God from dissolution.

THE SEAL OF TRUTH

Relative to the previous five, this commandment is the "seal of truth,"[4] the real measure of our relationship with God, the real measure of our loyalty to Him. Indeed, the

Hebrew word meaning "truth" (*emet*) is cognate to the word for "loyalty" (*ne'emanut*).

The "seal of truth" refers in Kabbalah to the *sefirah* of *yesod* ("foundation"), which corresponds in the body to the procreative organ, as noted earlier. Here, we are loyal ("true") to our spouse. In our relationship to God, our Divine groom, all of our pleasure and desire is permeated by His will and directed to Him alone.

"The righteous one is the foundation (*yesod*) of the world."[5] The righteous person of every generation, "the *one* [pillar] of the generation," is like the first human being, "Adam," before the sin. (Note that the Torah refers to both Adam and Eve as "Adam," as will be explained presently.)

Adam was created on the sixth, final day of creation, representing God's "seal of truth" with respect to all of creation that preceded that day. Truth is the realization of reaching the end, reaching the purpose of creation—Adam— the one and only created being capable of revealing God on earth.

Initially, Adam was the hidden "unconscious" of all creation, the initial *back* of creation. Adam was created as Siamese twins, with Eve at his back.[6] Just as Eve was the initial, unconscious side of Adam, so was Adam the initial unconscious side of the world, its *raison d'être*.

To Walk Behind God

Many verses of the Torah speak of serving God by "walking *after* ['behind'] Him," alluding to the sixth constant commandment of the Torah, "and you shall not stray *after* your hearts and *after* your eyes...." By not straying *after*, we come to walk *after* God in perfect loyalty to Him.[7]

Furthermore, this commandment includes the injunction against searching for God in "paths" other than the ways of the Torah.[8] Although these paths may lure us with the promise of excitement or more immediate spiritual gratification, if we remain true to our ideals we will focus our minds and hearts solely on God as He has made himself accessible to us, so to speak, through the "path" or lifestyle of the Torah. The Torah then teaches us how to properly meet the challenge of finding God in all aspects of reality.

REAR GUARD

Since the foe prefers to attack from behind,[9] trying to catch one off guard, this commandment is placed "behind" the consciousness, as a protective rear guard or background force field. Furthermore, "forward" and "backward" are often taken to indicate in Kabbalah "the desired" and "the undesired" (or "less-desired"). If we fulfill the first five commandments, we are assured in this sixth that the foreign enticements of this world will truly be "behind" us, which is why the verse is phrased, "And you shall not stray *after* [literally, 'behind'] your heart and *after* ['behind'] your eyes."[10]

Foreign enticements often distract us from what is truly meaningful in life and as a result we squander our energy, not allowing our lives to be as productive as they could be.[11] If we are truly devoted to God, we will desire to make our lives productive, or "potent." Rather than wasting our time and talents on things that add nothing to, and often even detract from the overall awareness of God in the world, we aspire to imbue all our actions with mindful purpose and drive in fulfilling God's will and heightening the world's awareness of Him.

SUNSET

As *front* and *back* correspond to east and west, they symbolize sunrise and sunset in the consciousness of the soul.

As our "sun," our clarity of mind, rises on the horizon of our consciousness, we are to unify God, the merciful Creator of the universe with the verse "Hear, O Israel...."

The idiom for "sunset" in Hebrew is literally "the coming of the sun." The sun penetrates the horizon, as it were, alluding to the secret in Kabbalah of the marital union of the *sefirah* of *yesod*, the *back* or west, with the *sefirah* of *malchut*. Malchut ("kingdom") is referred to as the *Shechinah* ("Divine Presence"), of which it is said, "the Divine Presence is in the west."[12] In the next chapter, we will see that *malchut* corresponds to prayer, the inner spiritual reality of "Living in Divine Space." In particular, it is the *back* or west, the commandment to guard one's mind to ever remain loyal to one's spouse, which unites with the commandment of prayer. For this reason, we are taught that "the hour of prayer is the hour of battle,"[13] the battle against foreign thoughts that attempt to bombard the mind especially during the time of prayer.

CHAPTER NINE

Prayer

ואני תפלה...

...And I am prayer

—Psalms 109:4

CHAPTER NINE

Prayer

Inside our meditative sanctuary is the consciousness of:

ואני תפלה...

...And I am prayer.[1]

The commandment to pray aspires to be, in effect, the seventh[2] constant commandment, although the Torah does not specifically define it as such.

CONSTANT PRAYER

Jewish law has specific guidelines as to how often one should pray. It is interesting to note the development of these guidelines. According to many authorities, prayer is not counted as one of the 613 commandments of the Written Torah.[3] In contrast, other authorities contend that indeed, one of the Torah's 613 commandments is that we pray to God, but that this obligation applies only when we find ourselves in need or trouble.[4] Yet others maintain that the Written Torah requires us to pray every day.[5]

73

The Oral Torah and Jewish custom, however, expand the obligation of prayer to three times daily for men and twice for women.[6] And finally, the sages of the Talmud voice the sentiment that: "Would that one pray the whole day, continuously."[7]

In this statement, the sages say that the ideal state of consciousness is constant prayer. Thus, we see that the service of prayer as an explicit commandment is in the "suspended state" of "becoming" a constant commandment, a full-time component of Jewish consciousness.[8]

TRANSCENDING SELF-AWARENESS

Even the consciousness produced by "Living in Divine Space," refined and ideal though it may be, is still *self-consciousness*. We are still aware of ourselves as we inhabit our sanctuary. The ultimate state of being, however, is for us to be so aware of the absolute dependence of all reality on the Godliness pulsating through it that we lose our awareness of self altogether, instead becoming only aware of everything as being (to one degree or another) a manifestation of God.

As long as we have not reached this level of consciousness we still experience ourselves and everything else as separate from God. In this state of consciousness we must "pray," that is, offer to God the consciousness we have been able to create in our meditative space. According to the Talmud,[9] prayer corresponds to (and is the inner dimension of) the sacrificial offerings of the Temple. In prayer, we offer ourselves to God. King David's statement "and I am prayer," may thus be read as "and my '*I*' is my offering [in prayer]."[10]

THE POINT WITHIN

This commandment is the point of self-consciousness situated in the middle of the six-sided cube of Divine-consciousness we have outlined. Relative to the other six commandments, prayer is the geometric central point of the cube, the experience of being "within" Divine consciousness while not yet having been totally absorbed in it.[11]

Prayer, as we have defined it here, is the ultimate expression of the Jewish faith. We believe that in sacrificing our consciousness of seeing the world as separate from God, we work toward creating a consciousness of unity with God, the ultimate goal of which is the revelation of His *absolute* infinity within the finite, physical world.

There are progressive dimensions in this revelation:

- Our super-rational faith in God (which we inherit from Abraham, Isaac, and Jacob) is itself a revelation of the infinite within the finite. Yet this revelation is still abstract, because the infinite is not *integrated* into the finite by our faith. However, such integration has been made possible by the Giving of the Torah at Mt. Sinai.

- Through Torah-study, our mind can grasp the infinite, and once it is grasped in the mind, this experience can filter down to the emotional and behavioral facets of life. Nonetheless, the infinite is still not evident in the physical world.

- Revelation of the infinite within the finite physical world, on a concrete level, is accomplished, little by little, by the fulfillment of the commandments. In the End of Days, the infinite will be fully revealed with the advent of the Messiah, the Resurrection of the Dead, and the subsequent World to Come.

This is the meaning of the statement of the Midrash:[12] "The Holy One, blessed be He, desired to have a dwelling place in lower reality," meaning that the consummation of creation will be when God is revealed within lower, physical reality itself.

Thus, when we say, "I am prayer," we are affirming our belief in the Divine revelation of the future, as well as expressing our desire to contribute our part toward the ultimate goal of all creation.[13]

THE ORDER

The following table summarizes all the seven commandments outlined above (the six constant commandments of the Torah and the seventh commandment that aspires to become constant, prayer):

above	belief in the existence of God
below	not believing in existence of other gods
front/ east	belief in the unity of God
right/ south	meditation on subjects that lead to love of God
left/ north	meditation on subjects that lead to fear of God
back/ west	shielding the mind from negative thoughts
sanctuary	prayer

The order in which we have presented the six constant commandments and prayer follows their logical order in terms of cause-effect relation:[14]

- We first become aware that God exists.
- This leads us to deny all pseudo-divinities.
- Once that is achieved, we see God in everything (and *as* everything).
- This leads us to love God.
- Our love brings us to fear separation from Him.
- This fear in turn inspires us to defend ourselves from distracting or confusing influences.
- Encompassed in the Divine space created by the six constant commandments, we stand before God in humility and pour out our hearts to Him in prayer.

CHAPTER TEN

Ever-Expanding Consciousness

CHAPTER TEN

Ever-Expanding
Consciousness

TO MEDITATE IS TO BUILD

The word for "meditation" in Hebrew (*hitbonenut*) is related to the verb "build" (*boneh*).

We begin the spiritual service of meditation by identifying a set of related Divine concepts and structuring them in our mind based upon one of the fundamental frames of reference of Kabbalah. The structure enables us to contemplate and understand in depth each of the concepts, their interdependencies and interrelationships. Once the concepts are well understood, the classic method of meditation is for us to reflect on the structure, now with the intention of animating its components with a living soul, before formal prayer.[1] Then, during prayer, we use the well-structured concepts as a method of enhancing our ever-unfolding and developing "face-to-face" relationship with God.[2] In prayer, we elevate and offer to God the body and soul of our meditation, and God, in return, inspires us with the insight and power to bring our meditation into our personal life.

A building consists of more than a skeletal frame. In meditation we must continually add more stones, bricks, mortar, etc. in order to strengthen and decorate the basic structure. Each layer adds in its own way to the overall potential of the meditation and to its astounding beauty. This, of course, implies a heightened appreciation for the beauty of the Torah itself, the Divine blueprint of creation in all of its splendor. All of this serves to increase the power of the meditation to affect the soul, the mind, and life in general.

The most apt model for this structure is the Jerusalem of the future.

THE JERUSALEM OF THE FUTURE

Of the Jerusalem of the future, it is written:

פרזות תשב ירושלם...
ואני אהיה לה נאם ה' חומת אש סביב
ולכבוד אהיה בתוכה.

*"Jerusalem will be settled as a city without walls....
And I," declares GOD, "will be a wall of fire around it,
and I will be a glory inside it."*[3]

First, it appears that Jerusalem will be "a city without walls." No walls will be able to contain it, neither will it need walls for protection. However, God then declares that He

Himself will be Jerusalem's "wall of fire." The teaching is clear: physical walls will not be necessary, because Jerusalem will become Divine space with God around it and God within it.

The Divine "wall of fire" is neither static nor stationary; eternally alive, it continuously expands. As the Midrash tells us: "Jerusalem will in the future expand to cover all the Land of Israel, and the Land of Israel will expand to cover the whole world." [4]

The nature of Divine space is to at once define the boundaries of our consciousness while simultaneously causing our consciousness to expand until it contains the entire cosmos. The sages refer to this phenomenon as "a boundless inheritance,"[5] based on God's promise to Jacob: "You shall break forth to the west, and to the east, and to the north, and to the south."[6]

SIX ASCENDING LEVELS OF HOLINESS

The sages speak of ten ascending levels of holiness that God created in the world. These levels begin with the holiness of the Land of Israel and ascend to the holiness of the innermost chamber of the Temple, the Holy of Holies.[7] Of the ten, six stand out in particular:[8]

1. the Land of Israel
2. the walled cities of Israel
3. the City of Jerusalem
4. the Temple Mount
5. the Temple

6. the Holy of Holies

In meditation, we may picture ourselves as ascending a ladder from level to level. These six levels themselves may be seen to correspond to the six constant commandments of the Torah, as we shall presently explain. We ascend to the apex of consciousness of the Divine space encompassing us, stand in a selfless state of prayer (the seventh commandment, which follows the six automatically) in the Holy of Holies (as the High Priest did on *Yom Kippur*), and then turn to experience our consciousness expanding to encompass the entire Land of Israel and the entire universe:

1. The Jewish people were commanded, upon entering the Land of Israel, to first purify the land from all idolatry.[9] This is the purification of the very ground of the Land of Israel, the direction of *below*, corresponding to the second of the six constant commandments.

2. The walled cities of Israel are those settlements physically protected from foreign invasion. In the soul, they correspond to the consciousness of the sixth constant commandment to shield/protect one's mind from foreign/negative thoughts, the direction of the *back*.

3. In Kabbalah and Hassidic thought, the name "Jerusalem" (*Yerushalayim*) is read "complete fear/awe" (*shleimut hayirah*). Melchizedek, who lived in the time of Abraham, had called the city *Shalem*, meaning "complete,"[10] but Abraham called it *yirah*, "awe."[11] The name *Yerushalayim* is a composite of the two, with "awe" preceding "complete." This clearly corresponds to the fifth of the constant commandments, the commandment to fear God, and the direction of *left*.

4. Abraham asked God for the area[12] where the Temple would stand—that is, the Temple Mount—and referred to the Temple-to-be as a "mountain" (*har*).[13] In Kabbalah and Hassidism, "mountain" symbolizes great love, the Divine attribute personified by Abraham. This, then, alludes to fourth of the constant commandments, the commandment to love God, and the direction of *right*.

5. Jacob called the Temple-to-be the "house" (*bayit*), and this is its name forever (*Beit HaMikdash* or "House of Sanctuary").[13] Inside the Temple, the Jewish soul experienced the absolute unity of God, reaching the level of consciousness associated with the soul of Jacob/Israel. This corresponds to direction of *front*, and the second of the constant commandments, the commandment to unify God, as we proclaim in the *Shema*: "Hear, O *Israel*, GOD is our God; GOD is one."[14]

6. In the Holy of Holies, God's very essence is revealed. Above even the four-letter Name of God, which we unite with His Name *Elokim* in proclaiming the *Shema*, is His very essence, expressed in the first word of the Ten Commandments—*Anochi* ("I am"). Here, the kernel essence of the first of the constant commandments, grasped in the simple, perfect faith of every (simple) Jew, transcends even the (relatively intellectually oriented) consciousness of the *Shema*.

In summary:[15]

above	Holy of Holies
front/east	Temple
right/south	Temple Mount
left/north	Jerusalem
below	Land of Israel
back/west	Walled cities
sanctuary	Prayer

CHAPTER ELEVEN

Living in Divine Space

הנה מקום אתי....

Behold, there is a place with Me...

—Exodus 33:21

CHAPTER ELEVEN

Living in Divine Space

"HE IS THE PLACE OF THE WORLD"

In conclusion, to appreciate in greater depth the dynamic nature of our meditative Divine space, we turn to the concept of space itself, which in Hebrew is often synonymous with "place" (*makom*).

Speaking to Moses, God says:

הנה מקום אתי.

Behold, there is a place with Me.[1]

The sages interpret this statement to mean: "He is the place of the world; the world is not His place."[2] Moreover, the sages use the word for "space/place"—*Makom*—to describe God Himself, the Omnipresent One.[3]

The Kabbalah takes this metaphor further, explaining that before the creation of the universe only God's infinite light existed, allowing no place or space for created worlds to exist. In order to begin the creative process, God "contracted" His infinite light, thereby creating a vacant space in which all created reality could come into existence.[4]

We may thus identify God Himself, the Omnipresent One, as the "higher space," in contrast to the apparent vacuum or "womb" in which creation exists, the "lower space."

In particular, each of these two "spaces" possesses two dimensions, four in all:

The higher, Divine space may refer either to God's very essence or to His transcendent light that encompasses all of creation. In Kabbalah, His transcendent light is identified with His will to create, also referred to as His "Name" that preceded creation.[5]

The lower space includes the apparent vacuum of creation. It also includes the "ray" of Divine creative energy that permeates the vacuum—God's immanent light.

To experience the omnipresence of God's very essence is to experience the ultimate, absolute truth that only God exists—"there is no other besides Him"[6]—to know that we are naught.

To experience His transcendent light, His will to create (as ever encompassing every point of reality), is to experience God's infinite goodness and how all of creation is no more than an expression of His will to be good to all.

To experience God's immanent light is to experience His Divine Providence in every facet of one's life.

To experience the apparent vacuum in which creation takes place is to experience existential distance from the apparently absent Creator and to long to "discover" His presence and become close to Him.

In summary:

level of reality		experience
upper space	God's essence	"there is nothing other than Him"
	God's transcendent light	God's infinite goodness
lower space	God's immanent light	Divine Providence
	the apparent vacuum of creation	distance from God and longing to be close to Him

THE MEANING OF SPACE

Why did God create space? The lowest of the four levels of space just described was created in order to make room for the existence of created beings possessing independent self-consciousness. At this level, space implies "separation," both of creation from its Creator and of one created being from another.

The next, higher level of space allows for relationship and sincere concern of one created being for the other. Here, space is experienced as a continuum of elementary particles of force, as gravitons, that bind reality together.

Yet above that, space is the union of the created in the Creator in absolute love.

Finally, space is no more than the essence of the Creator Himself.[7]

When we meditate on the space that surrounds us—visualizing and integrating into our consciousness the six constant commandments of the Torah as the parameters of that space—we cause our consciousness of space to expand and rise from level to level. We begin by feeling far from God, but the sense of distance implied by space gradually becomes converted into an experience of spontaneous gravitation to God. We feel encompassed in the embrace of His love, ultimately, becoming truly one with Him, the only true existence.

Supplementary
Essays

1

Seeking God[1]

בכל לבי דרשתיך.

"With all my heart I seek You."[2]

This is the verse that Rabbi Dovber of Lubavitch[3] chose to inscribe on the title page of his *Treatise on Meditation*. From this it is clear that meditation is seeking God with all one's heart.

Three idioms appear in the Bible describing the soul's quest for God: to "seek" or "search for" God (*doresh Havayah*), to "request" or "ask for" God (*mevakesh Havayah*), and to "wait for" or "expect" God (*meyachel leHavayah*). In Kabbalah, we are taught[4] that each of these three idioms describes a different experience of the soul in its quest for God. The three different experiences correspond to the states of consciousness of the three spiritual worlds: *Beriah* ("Creation"), *Yetzirah* ("Formation"), and *Asiyah* ("Action").

---

1. See p. 3.

2. Psalms 119:10.

3. Rabbi Dovber Shneuri, the second Rebbe of *Chabad*-Lubavitch (1773-1827).

4. See *Likutei Levi Yitzchak* on *Tanya*, *Igeret Hakodesh* 24.

The consciousness of the world of *Beriah* is that of pure thought or in-depth meditation, seeking God in one's mind and heart.

The consciousness of the world of *Yetzirah* is that of communing with God, speaking to Him directly in prayer or indirectly through the study of His Torah and taking counsel with a true Torah sage.[5]

The consciousness of the world of *Asiyah*, the world farthest removed from the experience of God's presence, is that of waiting for and expecting Divine revelation. While devoting our lives to positive, constructive deeds (the commandments of the Torah) we wait for God to come to us, feeling initially so far away from Him that we are unable to approach Him directly, in thought or word. Our waiting for God (while involved in positive action) does in fact arouse Him to come to us, and upon feeling His presence we then turn to Him in prayer and meditation.

In summary:

to seek or search for God	*Beriah*	meditating on God
to request or ask for God	*Yetzirah*	communicating with God
to wait for or expect God	*Asiyah*	waiting for God

---

5. The idiom "to seek GOD" appears in the context of those who came to Moses' tent to request the word of God from his mouth (Exodus 33:7). Rebecca also went "to seek GOD" (Genesis 25:22), and God answered her either through an angel (*Bereishit Rabbah* 63:7), or through Noah's son Shem (according to a second opinion in the same Midrash and to Rashi), or through Abraham (according to Ibn Ezra).

The full verse quoted above reads: "With all my heart I seek You, let me not stray from Your commandments." In seeking God with all our heart, we realize that our search must take place in the context of God's commandments, His instructions and guidelines to us where and how to find Him. This is in exact accord with the meditation presented here, the search for God within the context of the Divine space created by our conscious fulfillment of the six constant commandments of the Torah, from which we never want to stray.

The literal translation of the word for "stray" in the verse is "err," implying the straying of the mind or the entering into a mistaken state of consciousness with regard to the commandments, as explained by the classic commentaries on the text.[6] This relates in particular to the constant commandments of the Torah, the duties of the heart and mind, whose fulfillment is retaining continual, unerring consciousness of their truth (God exists, God is one, etc.), and responding, emotionally, in our heart to the truth we conceive in our mind.

In the Torah, the word for "to err" or "error" (*shegagah*) refers particularly to believing in or worshiping idols.[7] Idolatry is the general mis-focus and mistake of the mind and the heart. The purpose of all of the constant commandments of the Torah, the focus of our meditation, is

---

6. See *Metzudat David ad loc.*

7. Of the 21 times the root appears in the Torah, the highest concentration of the root is in *parashat Shelach*, where it appears 9 times in 8 verses (Numbers 15:22-29), all in reference to the "error" of idolatry.

to properly orient our mind and heart in order to keep even the slightest trace of idolatry from entering our consciousness.

Another indication that "to err" relates to meditation (i.e., that proper, Torah-oriented meditation is the correction of erroneous mentalities), is that the two-letter sub-root or "gate" (*shaar*) of "err" (*shin gimel*) is related to the two-letter sub-root of "comprehension" (*sin gimel*). "To comprehend" in Hebrew means as well "to reach" and "to achieve," and so "to err" means "to stray" from the path, to lose one's way and so, to become unable to reach and achieve one's goal.

In Kabbalah, we are taught that erroneous mentality derives, ultimately, from an unrectified character, primarily from an unbalanced sense of ego. One of the most fundamental teachings of the Ba'al Shem Tov[8] is that before we fulfill a commandment, we must experience a certain measure of "upliftedness" or "highness of spirit," for otherwise we will have no motivation to initiate the performance of the commandment. But as soon as we begin to act (or meditate, in the case of the six constant commandments of the Torah), and most surely, when we have successfully fulfilled a commandment, we must consider ourselves to be nothing, realizing that in truth, only by virtue of the grace and power of God did we accomplish what we accomplished. The greatest character flaw is the reversal of the senses of highness of spirit and lowliness of spirit. If we initially feel lowly, we will lack the stamina and willpower to take the initiative to get up and do. This is especially true with

---

8. *Keter Shem Tov* 393.

regard to the most important missions of life that affect not only ourselves but the entire community, of which is said, "In a place where there are no men, try to be a man!"[9] If we feel high after succeeding in performing a good deed, this is the essence of arrogance.

All of this is alluded to in the two-letter sub-root of "to err"—*shin gimel*. The shin stands for *shiflut*—"lowliness of spirit"; the *gimel* stands for *gavhut*—"highness of spirit." When this is the order of the expressions of our ego, from low before acting to high while and after acting, we are caught up in an existential syndrome of "error." The rectified character is alluded to by the reverse order: the *gimel* of *gavhut* precedes the *shin* of *shiflut*, forming the two-letter sub-root of the word for "approach" (*hagashah*). When we possess the proper measure of *gavhut* necessary to initiate a good deed and then know how to attribute the deed to God alone, we approach God in true *shiflut*.

This teaching is especially important in our Divine service of meditation. If the thought enters the mind, "Who are you to meditate on Godliness, to consciously seek God in your mind and heart? You are far from God; your mind and heart are impure; God will never enter them!" we must know how to assume the proper measure of *gavhut* to overcome and negate this thought. There is no greater merit than experiencing Godliness in meditation, loving and standing in awe of our Creator, so after meditating, the experience of *shiflut* must be adopted in full. We have seen that for this reason, as soon as we have created around ourselves the

---

9. *Avot* 2:5.

Divine Space of our meditation, we must immediately enter into a state of prayer, nullifying our ego entirely, pouring out our heart to God.

The initial letters of the first three words of the verse, "With all my heart I seek You" (בכל לבי דרשתיך) permute to spell the word for "alone" (לבד), as in the verse, "And Jacob remained alone [לבדו], and a man wrestled with him until dawn."[10] In our search for God, we are alone—not alone by ourselves but alone with God, in perfect faith that, although we do not see Him, He is certainly here with us, waiting and encouraging us to seek and find Him. By the power of our simple faith in God, we are able to overcome the archangel of Esau, who, in the form of our own evil inclination, wrestles with us in the solitude of our meditation.

The initial letters of the next three words of the verse, "Do not let me stray from Your commandments" (אל תשגני ממצוותיך) permute to spell the word for "truth" (אמת). Truth lies in the commandments of the Torah (the essence of truth, "There is no truth but the Torah"[11]). If we stray from the commandments of the Torah, we stray from the truth, and our meditation, our desire to seek God, falls into illusion. In our meditation we beseech God, "Let us not stray from the truth of Your commandments!"

Together, the initial letters of the entire verse spell "truth alone" (אמת לבד), whose own initial letters (אמת לבד) spell *Kel* (אל), the Name of God used in juxtaposition with the word "truth," as in the phrase "a God of truth" (אל אמת).

---

10. Genesis 32:25.

11. *Eichah Rabbah*, introduction 2.

The numerical values of the two words for "truth" and "alone" are each a square (i.e., perfect, in Kabbalah) number. The word for "truth" (אמת) equals $441 = 21^2$ and "alone" (לבד) equals $36 = 6^2$. With regard to the two square roots, 21 is the triangle of 6 (the sum of all numbers from 1 to 6). The numerical value of the word for "truth" itself (אמת) in the ordinal numbering system (the 22 letters of the Hebrew alphabet numbered from 1 to 22) is $36 = 6^2$, the value of the word for "alone" (לבד) in the normative numbering system. In the reduced numbering system (in which each letter is reduced to one of the numerals from 1 to 9), both words equal 9—"truth" equals "alone." 9 is the value of the letter *tet* in the Hebrew alphabet. Thus, "truth alone" reduces to two *tet*'s, alluding to the first two letters of the word for the head *tefilin*—*totafot*—we wear in our morning prayers. The head *tefilin* strengthen our intellect to focus our meditation on God alone while retaining continual consciousness of the constant commandments of the Torah. This continual consciousness is reflected in the requirement of the *halachah* that so long as one is wearing *tefilin*, one is not to take his mind off them.

2

The Ways of God[1]

The Torah's commandments are called "the ways of GOD."[2]

The numerical value of "the ways of GOD" (דרכי י-הוה) is 260, 10 times 26, the value of God's essential Name *Havayah* (the word for "the ways of" [דרכי] equals 234 = 9 times 26). This teaches us that "the ways of GOD," the commandments of the Torah, entail the full and ultimate revelation of God in the world, for 10 times a number alludes, in Kabbalah, to its full revelation in all the ten powers of the soul (which correspond to the ten supernal *sefirot*, the channels by which God created the world).

God chose Abraham to be the first Jew (before the Giving of the Torah with its 613 explicit commandments to Israel at Mt. Sinai), because He knew that Abraham would keep "the way of GOD to do charity and justice."[3] This is the first and only appearance of the idiom "the way of GOD" (or "the ways of GOD") in the Five Books of Moses. From this

---

1. See p. 4.

2. See Genesis 18:19; Judges 2:22; 2 Samuel 22:22; 2 Kings 21:22; Jeremiah 5:4-5; Hosea 14:10; Psalms 18:22, 25:4, 138:5; 2 Chronicles 17:6; see also *Ner Mitzvah veTorah Or*, introduction (2b).

3. Genesis 18:19.

we learn that "to do charity and justice" is the all-inclusive "way of GOD."

The Torah is called "the Tree of Life."[4] In this imagery, practicing "charity and justice" are the trunk of the tree, and the 613 commandments its branches. The six constant commandments of the Torah, the duties of the heart, are the roots of the tree. The commandment to love one's fellow as oneself is the sap, the life-force, that flows from the roots up the trunk into all the branches of the tree.

branches	all the 613 commandments of the Torah
trunk	practicing charity and justice; "the way of GOD"
sap	loving one's fellow as oneself
roots	the six constant commandments of the Torah

The numerical value of the phrase "the way of GOD to do charity and justice" (דרך י-הוה לעשות צדקה ומשפט) is 1690 = 26 times 65. 26 is the value of God's essential Name *Havayah* as it is written; 65 is the value of the Name as it is read (*Adni*). Thus, 1690 is the product of God's concealed and revealed dimensions. (Throughout the Torah, whenever a word is read not as it is written, its written form represents its concealed dimension whereas its verbal expression represents its revealed dimension.) 26 = 2 times 13; 65 = 5 times 13; their product, 1690, thus equals 10 times 13^2. As we have seen above, 13 is the numerical value of "one" (אחד) and "love"

---

4. Proverbs 3:18.

(אהבה). 1690 is thus perfect unity and love—13²—ten times over, i.e., revealed in all the ten powers of the soul.

"The way of GOD" (דרך י-הוה) equals 250, the numerical value of the word for "candle" (נר). Every commandment of the Torah is a candle, as explicitly stated in Proverbs (6:23): "For a commandment is a candle...." The purpose of the candle is to illuminate the way in our search for God, as it is said in Psalms,[5] "Your word is a candle to my foot...." A candle is meant to shine at night, i.e., in a state of darkness, a state of concealment of Divine light, the general state of this world. The commandments were given to reveal God's great, infinite light in the darkness. For this reason, "candle," 250, equals "great light" (אור גדול), as in the words of Isaiah,[6] "The people walking in darkness saw great light." Every small candle is indeed a contraction or condensation of great, infinite light, the light of the Torah in every one of its commandments: "For a commandment is a candle and the Torah is light."

Because the commandments are "ways," the legal body of the Torah is referred to as *halachah*, from the word for "walking" (*halichah*).[7] Torah-oriented life is never static; it is always dynamic, always progressing, moving ahead. Every one of the commandments of the Torah is a vector force

---

5. Psalms 119:105.

6. Isaiah 9:1.

7. Cf. the sages' statement: "It was taught by Elijah: Whoever studies Torah laws every day is assured of life in the World to Come, for it is said: 'The ways of the world are his' [Habakkuk 3:6]. Do not read 'ways' [*halichot*] but 'Torah laws' [*halachot*]" (*Tanna d'vei Eliahu Zuta* 2; *Megilah* 28b; *Nidah* 73a).

directed toward God. The very word for "commandment" (*mitzvah*) means "togetherness," for each commandment is a way to come together with God. This is especially the case with regard to the six constant commandments of the Torah, the duties of the heart, for each is a conscious vector force of the mind and heart that impels us to come close and unite with God.

3

Pouring Out the Heart[1]

The service of the heart in prayer is, figuratively, pouring out one's heart to God. In the words of the prophet Jeremiah: "Pour out your heart like water in the presence of the countenance of GOD."[2]

The idiom of pouring out one's heart like water alludes to the pouring of water on the altar of the Holy Temple on the festival of *Sukot*,[3] "the time of our happiness."[4] When God separated the lower waters from the higher waters on the second day of creation, we are told that the lower waters cried, "We, too, want to be close to God [as are the higher waters]."[5] While not alleviating the frustration of the lower waters entirely, God did promise them that they would come close to Him on *Sukot* with the pouring of the water on the altar. Thus, in the performance of this commandment, the bitterness of the lower waters became converted into joy.

---

1. See p. 6.

2. Lamentations 2:19.

3. *Sukot* is the one time of the year when we physically build a Divine Space around us, in the form of the *sukah*.

4. Liturgy, festival *Amidah*.

5. *Tikunei Zohar* 80a.

This is precisely in accord with the nature of the spiritual service of the heart (in prayer). We are taught that the ideal state of spiritual equilibrium in the heart is one of "crying on one side [the left side] of the heart and being joyful on the other side [the right side] of the heart."[6] Experiencing our existential distance from God, we cry; experiencing coming close to Him, we are filled with joy. When we pour out our heart to God in prayer, we experience simultaneously the lower waters' bitterness as they cry out to God and how their crying is converted into joy as they are offered to God on the spiritual altar of our heart.

The sum of the numerical values of the two words for "crying" (בכיה, 37) and "joy" (חדוה, 23) in the above saying is 60, the product of the two letters that form the word "heart" (לב; ל = 30, ב = 2, 30 times 2 = 60). Thus, as stated, the presence of the two emotions of crying and joy in the heart, in perfect balance, is indicative of a rectified Jewish heart.

---

6. *Zohar* 2:255a.

4

The Name of God[1]

In Hebrew, we refer to God as *Hashem*, literally, "The Name."[2]

The word "name" (שם) means, as well, "noun" or "word" in general. This is a further indication that God has given Himself to us in every word of the Torah.

Similar to the relative nature of the flower and the bouquet discussed before,[3] we are taught that the entire Torah (The Five Books of Moses)—all of its letters, words, verses, etc., together as one—is in fact one great Name of

---

1. See p. 12.

2. We find God referred to as *Hashem* explicitly in the Torah text (Deuteronomy 28:58):

...ליראה את השם הנכבד והנורא הזה את ה׳ אלהיך

...to fear this glorious and awesome Name, GOD, your God.

Significantly, the numerical value of the phrase "to fear this glorious and awesome Name," 1358, is identical with that of the second sentence of the *Shema* (added by the sages): "Blessed be the Name of His glorious kingdom forever and ever" (**ברוך שם כבוד מלכותו לעולם ועד**). Both phrases are composed of 6 words and 24 letters!

3. p. 12.

God,[4] for, ultimately, "the Torah and God are one,"[5] as God and His Name are one.[6]

In particular, we are taught in Kabbalah that all of the words of the Torah can be divided into four categories, each category a different level of revelation of the Name of God:

The first category is the 1820 explicit appearances of God's essential Name, *Havayah*, in the Torah. (1820 = 70 times 26; 70 is the numerical value of the word for "secret" [סוד] and 26 is the value of the Name *Havayah*; 70 times 26 thus encapsulates the phrase, "the secret of *Havayah*.")

The second category is all of the other explicit Names of God that appear in the Torah, excluding the essential Name, *Havayah*, which when written are forbidden to be erased.[8]

The third category is all of the words in the Torah that explicitly refer to God, connoting Him or describing His attributes, such as "the merciful One" (*rachum*).

The fourth category includes all the remaining words of the Torah, whose meanings, whether manifestly "good" or "bad," all contain the concealed presence of God and His Divine Providence.

---

4. Introduction to Nachmanides' commentary on the Torah

5. *Zohar* 1:24a.

6. *Pirkei d'Rabbi Eliezer* 3.

7. Psalms 25:14.

8. *Mishneh Torah, Yesodei HaTorah* 6:2.

These four categories themselves correspond to the four letters of God's essential Name, *Havayah*: the explicit Names *Havayah* correspond to the first letter, the *yud*, the initial point and flash of wisdom (*chochmah*) in which the whole Name is included, as it is said, "*Havayah* in wisdom...."[9] All the other explicit Names of God correspond to the first *hei* of *Havayah*, the level of understanding (*binah*) that never parts from wisdom.[10] The connotations and Divine attributes correspond to the *vav* of *Havayah*, the letter that explicitly refers to the six Divine emotive attributes. All other words correspond to the final *hei* of *Havayah*, God's kingdom (*malchut*) on earth, where His presence is at once concealed—allowing for the appearance of the mundane and even evil—and simultaneously revealed in His Divine Providence over all.

In summary, all of the words of the Torah combine to become one Name of God. First, they are seen to fall into four distinct categories, corresponding to the four letters of the Name *Havayah*, which join together to become one. Finally, they combine as *one* long word composed of hundreds of thousands of letters (without spaces between the words, as they presently appear in the Torah), one essential Name of God with no relation to the individual words at all. This final revelation is the "new Torah" that the Messiah will reveal to the world, the revelation that "God is all and all is God."

---

9. Proverbs 3:19.

10. *Zohar* 3:4a.

Relative to the four distinct categories of words that combine to form the secret of God's Name, the entire Torah as one, long Name of God manifests the fifth level above the four, corresponding to the tip of the *yud*.

To summarize:

tip of *yud*	the Torah as one, long Name of God
yud	the Name *Havayah*
hei	other Names of God
vav	words that connote God
hei	all other words in the Torah

5

Sinai Past and Present[1]

*You were shown to know that GOD is God, there is
no other besides Him.*[2]

This verse is followed by its complementary verse:

*You shall know this day and take to heart that
GOD is God in the heavens above and on the earth
below, there is no other.*[3]

The first verse refers to the revelation of the Giving of
the Torah to Israel at Mt. Sinai. The second, complementary
verse refers to the service of meditation, the ongoing
commandment to relive and re-experience the revelation of
Sinai, to "know this day take to heart [i.e., meditate in mind
and heart] that GOD is God in the heavens above and on the
earth below, there is no other." In Kabbalah, the first verse is
an experience of "straight" or "direct" light (*or yashar*), a
revelation from above. The second, complementary verse is
an experience of "returning" or "reflected" light (*or chozer*),
the service of the soul below.

---

1. See p. 13.

2. Deuteronomy 4:35.

3. *Ibid.* 4:39.

Let us meditate on the two verses in their original Hebrew:

אתה הראת לדעת כי ה' הוא האלהים
אין עוד מלבדו.

וידעת היום והשבת אל לבבך כי ה' הוא האלהים
בשמים ממעל ועל הארץ מתחת אין עוד.

The first verse contains 10 words and the second verse contains 16 words. Together, they contain 26 words, the numerical value of the Name *Havayah*. The 10 words of the first verse correspond to the first letter of the Name *Havayah*, the *yud*, whose numerical value is 10. The 16 words of the second verse correspond to the last three letters of the Name *Havayah*—*hei, vav, hei*—whose combined numerical value is 16.

In particular, the 5 Hebrew words that mean, "You shall know today and take to heart" correspond to the first *hei* of *Havayah*, whose numerical value is 5; the 6 next Hebrew words, which mean "that GOD is God in the heavens above," correspond to the *vav* of *Havayah*, whose numerical value is 6; and the final 5 Hebrew words, which mean "and on the earth below, there is no other," correspond to the final *hei* of *Havayah*.

Divine revelation from above, reflects the *yud* of *Havayah*, which corresponds to the *sefirah* of *chochmah* and the sense of sight ("You were shown…"). This is especially so with regard to the revelation of the Giving of the Torah to

Israel, for "the Torah issues from *chochmah*,"[4] and this revelation is expressed in the *Ten* Commandments, the numerical value of the *yud*.

"You shall know this day and take to heart" refers explicitly to the Divine service of meditation, *hitbonenut*, from the word *binah*, "understanding," the first *hei* of *Havayah*.[5] The word for "take" to your heart (והשבת), literally reads "return" to your heart, alluding to returning light and to the Divine service of the heart to return to God, *teshuvah*. Indeed, the five letters of והשבת permute to spell תשובה, *teshuvah*.

Finally, "heavens above" and "earth below" correspond to the *vav* and the final *hei* of *Havayah*, respectively. The heavens symbolize the emotive attributes of the soul (the *vav* of *Havayah*), while the earth symbolizes the attribute of *malchut*, the "kingdom [of God on earth]" (the final *hei* of *Havayah*).

In the composition of the Torah text, almost all verses naturally divide into two segments or sentences (whose separation is indicated by the cantillation mark *etnachta*). The combined numerical value of the second halves of our two complementary verses—"there is no other besides Him" and "there is no other"—is 364 = 14 times 26 (the value of God's essential Name, *Havayah*) or 28 times 13 (the value of the

---

4. *Zohar* 2:121a.

5. "You shall *know*..." refers to *da'at*; the interdependence of *da'at* and *binah* is seen the sages' teaching that "If there is no *da'at*, there is no *binah*, and if there is no *binah*, there is no *da'at*" (*Avot* 3:17). "...and take to *heart*" refers to *binah*, as is stated in the *Zohar* (*Tikunei Zohar*, introduction [17a]): "*Binah* is the heart, and with it the heart understands."

word for "one," אחד). The combined numerical value of the first halves of the verses is 5005 = 13 times 385 (the value of *Shechinah* [שכינה], the Divine Presence, itself the "pyramid" of 10, that is, the sum of all squares from 1 to 10, as well as 7 times 55, the "triangle" of 10, that is, the sum of all numbers from 1 to 10). Both numbers, 364 and 5005 are multiples of 91, 7 times 13, the union of God's essential Name as it is written (*Havayah*, 26 = 2 times 13) and as it is read (*Adni*, 65 = 5 times 13).

In summary, we learn from the comparison of these two complementary verses that ideally, our life service of meditation on the unity and omnipresence of God is the soul's response to the awesome revelation of Divinity it once experienced, and whose impression remains with it, either in the forefront or the back of its consciousness. When the impression remains in the forefront of our consciousness, the service of meditation is easier; otherwise, it is harder. In either case, with the devoted, daily service of Divine meditation, every soul is able to find God.[6]

All Jewish souls stood at Mt. Sinai when the heavens opened and the Torah was given to Israel. All "saw the voices."[7] We all possess the impression of this experience in our (collective) unconscious. Some pure souls experience it directly in full consciousness, without the need to invest great spiritual effort in in-depth meditation. Most of us, however, need to make this investment, whose profit for the soul is infinite.

---

6. See *Tanya*, chapter 42.

7. Exodus 20:14.

The greater our efforts to meditate, to relive the experience of the Giving of the Torah to Israel at Mt. Sinai, the more we manifest in our souls "returning" or "reflected" light (*or chozer*), as explained above. In Kabbalah and Hassidism, we are taught that "reflected light returns to it's ultimate source," a source deeper in the essence of G-d's infinite light than the revealed source of G-d's "straight" or "direct" light (*or yashar*). Thus, the profit we gain by investing great spiritual effort in in-depth meditation exceeds the direct revelation that is given to those pure souls to whom the recollection of the Giving of the Torah comes naturally.

6

The Commandments of God[1]

The 613 commandments of the Torah can be categorized in various ways:

- positive (of which there are 248) and prohibitive (of which there are 365),
- to which *soul* they apply (e.g., everyone or only the king, the priests, etc.),
- at which *time* they apply (at all times or only when the Temple is standing, etc.),
- in which *place* they apply (everywhere or only in the Land of Israel, only in the Temple, etc.).

The four distinctions listed above correspond to the four letters of God's essential Name, *Havayah*. First, we will discuss the three last distinctions (soul, time, place), which correspond to the last three letters of the Name *Havayah* (*hei*, *vav*, *hei*). We will then return to the first distinction to see how it parallels the first letter (*yud*) of *Havayah*.

It is taught in Kabbalah and Hassidism that the question "who?" is associated with the *sefirah* of *binah*, which corresponds to the first *hei* of the Name *Havayah*.[2]

---

1. See p. 19.

2. *Zohar*, introduction.

Order in time is the secret of the six days of creation, which correspond to the six emotive *sefirot* and powers of the soul, from *chesed* to *yesod*, the *vav* of the Name *Havayah*.

Order or position in space is identified in Kabbalah with *malchut*, the final *hei* of the Name *Havayah*. The king is seen as occupying the middle point of space, his ministers around him, and so on.

The first, most essential distinction with regard to the commandments of the Torah, namely, their categorization into positive and prohibitive commandments (literally, *mitzvot aseih*, the "do's," and *mitzvot lo taaseih*, the "don'ts"), corresponds to the *yud*, the first letter of the Name *Havayah*. This correspondence can be seen from the verse, "You have made all with wisdom [*chochmah*, which corresponds to the *yud* of the Name *Havayah*]."[3] In *Sefer Yetzirah*,[4] it is stated that God created the sense of *asiyah*, "making" (as in the verse, "You have made…") or "doing" (from the root *aseih*, the root of the terms for the do's and the don'ts of the Torah) in the soul with the letter *yud*.

The sages teach us that in reality, even the prohibitive commandments of the Torah are also positive commandments. In the words of the Talmud, "He who sits and refrains from a forbidden act receives reward as though he performed a positive commandment."[5] Thus, "You have made" includes both that which God has visibly created as well as that which He has not created in external reality. His

---

3. Psalms 104:24.
4. 5:8.
5. *Kidushin* 39b.

free choice of what to do and what not to do derive, ultimately, from the same place and power in His being.

The numerical value of the *yud* is 10, which is seen to divide into two groups; in the terminology of Kabbalah, five *chasadim* (degrees of loving-kindness) and five *gevurot* (degrees of severity). The five *chasadim* are the origin of the 248 positive commandments of the Torah; the five *gevurot* are the origin of the 365 prohibitive commandments of the Torah. This division is clearly expressed in the Ten Commandments, in which all the commandments of the Torah, both positive and prohibitive and encapsulated. The ten were inscribed on the two Tablets of the Covenant in two parallel groups, five opposite five.

Thus, we see how every commandment of the Torah is a "commandment of GOD".[6] Each one brings us close and connects us to God by means of its own, special manifestation of each of the four letters of His essential Name, *Havayah*.

yud	positive or prohibitive	Divinity, origin of free choice in the soul	wisdom
hei	who	Soul	understanding
vav	when	Time	emotions
hei	where	Space	kingdom

---

6. Leviticus 4:2, etc.

7

The Commandments:
Spiritual and Physical[1]

All the 613 commandments of the Torah are intended to be performed physically; for this reason the commandments are referred to as "active commandments," *mitzvot ma'asiyot*. Even those commandments termed "the duties of the heart" must affect us on the physical plane. There must be some measurable physiological evidence, such as an augmented heartbeat, that we are performing these commandments.

Nonetheless, relative to the other *mitzvot ma'asiyot*, those commandments termed "the duties of the heart" are spiritual *mitzvot*. In general, the spiritual plane of existence and the physical plane unite in virtue of the "inter-inclusion" of one in the other, i.e., the physical in the spiritual and the spiritual in the physical. This is similar to the union of male and female, as taught in Kabbalah. (Relative to one another, "male" is spiritual while "female" is physical.) In marital relations, for the sake of bearing offspring, the female dimension present within the male must unite with the male dimension within the female.

---

1. See p. 19.

120

So it is too with regard to the commandments: The physical dimension included within the relatively spiritual commandments, "the duties of the heart," is the measurable physiological evidence that we are performing these *mitzvot*, as mentioned above. The spiritual dimension included within the *mitvot ma'asiyot* is the emotion of the heart with which we perform these *mitzvot*. All *mitzvot* are intended to be performed with the consciousness that in so doing we are fulfilling the will of God. The positive *mitzvot* are intended to be motivated by the emotion of love for God and the prohibitive *mitzvot* by the fear of God.

The physical dimension of "the duties of the heart" unites with the spiritual dimension of the *mitzvot ma'asiyot* of the Torah, just as in the union of male and female, as described above.

The meditation we have presented here—"Living in Divine Space"—intends to create a balanced "male" and "female" presence within the relatively "male" (spiritual) side of our being. Retaining the consciousness of "Living in Divine Space," we perform the *mitzvot ma'asiyot* of the Torah, thereby creating a balanced "male" and "female" presence within the relatively "female" (physical) side of our being.

Significantly, women are obliged to perform "the duties of the heart," but are not obliged to perform most of the time-dependent positive *mitzvot ma'asiyot* of the Torah. ("The duties of the heart" are constant commandments, not time-dependent.) Thus, both men and women are obliged to create in their being a well-balanced "male" (spiritual) side through meditation. On the other hand, men are more responsible than women to create in their being a balanced "female" (physical) side (which they accomplish by performing the time-dependent positive *mitzvot ma'asiyot*). In Kabbalah, it is explained that this is so for women are naturally "female," i.e., physically oriented, and thus require less work on their female side.

8

The All-Inclusive Commandments[1]

In a deep sense, the six continuous commandments are all-inclusive of all the 613 commandments of the Torah. In Psalms,[2] it is stated: "All of Your commandments are faith." The numerical value of the word for "faith" (*emunah*) is 102. Each of the six "duties of the heart," the six constant commandments of the Torah, is a commandment of faith. They all derive from the first, which is also the first of the Ten Commandments, the belief in the existence and providence of God. Simple faith in the existence of God is what brings us to contemplate His absolute unity, to love and fear Him, not to believe in any other god, and to guard our minds from thoughts that would sever us from our simple faith in Him.

Each of these commandments may thus be seen to encompass 102 of the Torah's 613 commandments. Six times 102 equals 612 (the value of the word for "covenant," *brit*, our eternal bond to God), to which we add the commandment of prayer, thus arriving at the full number of 613 commandments.

In particular, *emunah* is spelled אמונה, which can be read א מונה (*alef moneh*), "one [א = 1] counts [מונה]." "Counts"

---

1. See p. 19.
2. 119:86.

(*moneh*) equals 101, the numerical value of the word for "from nothing" (*mei-ayin*), as in the idiom, "something from nothing" (*yesh mei-ayin*). All numbers are no more than an enumeration of ones, all of which are ultimately reflections of the very same, original 1. Thus, the simple 1 of pure faith in "GOD is one" "counts" from itself—that is, "emanates"— 101 additional reflections or perspectives of the original, essential oneness. The 1 is the essence of the Divine "nothing"; the additional 101, an extension "*from* nothing."

"Living in Divine Space" is thus a meditation on the essence of the Divine nothing, from which all is created, beginning with the emanation of the 613 commandments of the Torah, the 613 "limbs" and "sinews" of the "image of God" that God emanated from His infinite light in order to create man "in His image." And so, each of the six *mitzvot* of faith encompasses 102.

The numerical value of the name of the first Jew, Abraham, is 248, the number of positive commandments in the Torah, corresponding to the 248 limbs of the human body. Abraham lived 175 years.[3] 175 is *emunah* (102) plus 73, the value of the word for "wisdom," *chochmah*. When another 73 is added to 175 we arrive at 248, Abraham. But, 5 times 73 equals 365, the number of prohibitive commandments in the Torah, corresponding to the 365 sinews or major blood vessels of the human body. Thus, 613 equals *emunah* and seven times *chochmah*. God created seven "wisdoms" in the world.[4] These themselves, as the seven branches of the

---

3. Genesis 25:7.

4. Based on Proverbs 9:1.

menorah in the sanctuary of the Holy Temple, are divided into two groups of two and five (as alluded to in the word for "gold," *zahav*, whose three letters, *zayin hei beit*, equal 7, 5, and 2, respectively, alluding to the equation: 7 = 5 plus 2).

The full number of the Torah's commandments, 613, thus equals 6 times *emunah*, with an additional 1, as well as *emunah* and seven times *chochmah*. This teaches us that the consummate manifestation of faith in God includes all seven wisdoms of creation. To be truly wise is to have perfect faith in God, the Creator.

9

The Six Cities of Refuge[1]

The *Sefer HaChinuch* refers, allegorically, to the six constant commandments of the Torah as "the six cities of refuge," designated to serve as refuge for those guilty of manslaughter. Their purpose was to rectify the faulty state of consciousness responsible for the individual's unintentional act of manslaughter.

Similarly, every Jew is instructed to correct his or her state of consciousness, remaining constantly conscious of God's presence, by entering the six constant commandments of the Torah and always remaining within the spiritual "space" they create.

There were three cities of refuge to the west of the Jordan River and three to the east. These two sets of three cities correspond to the two poles of Divine service expressed in the Book of Psalms as the directives to "turn from evil and do good."[2]

The three cities to the west, in the Land of Israel proper, correspond to the first, third, and fourth of the constant commandments: to believe in the existence of God; to believe and know His unity; and to love Him. (These three

---

1. See p. 20

2. Psalm 34:15.

are essentially positive in nature, "do good," characterizing the spiritual state of the Land of Israel proper.)

The three cities to the east of the Jordan correspond to the second, fifth, and sixth of the six commandments—not to believe in other gods, to fear God, and to shield one's mind from negative thoughts. (These three are essentially prohibitive in nature, "turn from evil"; the second and the sixth are explicitly prohibitive commandments, the fifth, "to fear God," although a positive commandment, is the spiritual power that motivates us to observe all of the 365 prohibitive commandments of the Torah, as has been explained. "Turning from evil" characterizes the spiritual state of the east bank of the Jordan River).

The order of the six constant commandments that we have presented throughout our discussion is the order given by Maimonides. We will take note of a significant mathematical phenomenon with regard to this order.

As stated, the first, third, and fourth of the six constant commandments are those that correspond to the three cities of refuge in the Land of Israel proper. $1^2 + 3^2 + 4^2 = 26$. 26 is the numerical value of God's essential Name, *Havayah*, which represents faith and love, the positivity that characterizes the Land of Israel.

The second, fifth, and sixth of the six constant commandments are those that correspond to the three cities of refuge in Transjordan. $2^2 + 5^2 + 6^2 = 65$. 65 is the numerical value of God's Name *Adni* (the way in which the Name *Havayah* is pronounced), which represents the fear of heaven and acceptance of the obligations of God's kingdom, the power that motivates us to "turn from evil," the characteristic property of the land on the east side of the Jordan.

The sum of the six numbers from 1 to 6 is 21, the numerical value of another one of God's holy Names, *Ekyeh*, "I Shall Be," the Name that God revealed to Moses at the Burning Bush, before the Exodus (with which He promised us that He will always be with us to redeem us from exile).

The number 21 appears in the famous series known in the secular world by the name of its discoverer, Leonardo Fibonacci, a medieval Italian mathematician, and in Kabbalah as "the series of love." The series begins with two 1's (or, equivalently, with 0 and 1). Every number in the series is the sum of the two previous numbers. 21 is the eighth number in the series: 1 1 2 3 5 8 13 21.... The division of 21 into 8 and 13 is known as the "golden section" of 21.

In our above analysis of the six constant commandments (in their natural order), the three commandments that correspond to the three cities of refuge in the Land of Israel (the three commandments to "do good"), 1, 3, and 4 = 8. The three commandments that correspond to the cities of refuge on the east side of the Jordan (the three commandments to "turn from evil"), 2, 5, and 6 = 13. This gives the golden section of 21. In each of the two groups, its middle number further divides it into the golden section: 8 divides into 3 (the middle number of 1, 3, and 4) and 5 (1 and 4); 13 divides into 5 (the middle number of 2, 5, and 6) and 8 (2 and 6).

This is the *only* possible way to so perfectly divide the six numbers from 1 to 6!

10

The Cube and Pascal's Triangle[1]

In Kabbalah, the significance of a cube is that it possesses 8 vertices (points), 12 lines, and 6 faces (areas), all of which add up to 26, the numerical value of God's essential Name, *Havayah*.[2]

As we have seen, Kabbalah understands the universe—both the physical universe and the parallel spiritual universe—as an ever-expanding cube. Indeed, the cube is a five-dimensional hypercube, composed of three spatial dimensions, a fourth dimension of time and a fifth dimension of "soul," or "morality" (its two extremes being "good" and "evil").

If we add the 1 volume of the cube to its 26 components (of point, line, and area) we arrive at a total number of 27 components, from dimension 0 (point) to dimension 3 (volume). 27 is 3 cubed. Let us continue to analyze multi-dimensional cubes:

- A zero-dimensional cube is a point. It possesses one single component, the point itself.
- A one-dimensional cube is a line. It possesses 3 components, two points and one line.

---

1. See p. 20.
2. *Likutei HaGra* at the end of *Sefer Yetzirah* (2:25b).

- A two-dimensional cube is a square. It possesses 9 components, 4 points, 4 lines and 1 area.
- The three-dimensional cube possesses 27 components, as enumerated above.

We see that the total number of components of the first four "cubes" follows a definite order: 1, 3, 9, 27—the powers of 3.

- The four-dimensional hypercube possesses 16 points, 32 lines, 24 areas, 8 volumes, and 1 four-dimensional whole, a total of 81 components—3 to the 4th power.
- The five-dimensional hypercube possesses 32 points, 80 lines, 80 areas, 40 volumes, 10 four-dimensional "volumes," and 1 five-dimensional whole, a total of 243 components—3 to the 5th power.
- And so *ad infinitum*.

Let us note that the number of points follows the order of the powers of 2, whereas the total number of components follows the order of the powers of 3.

As stated, of special importance is the five-dimensional hypercube, composed of 243 components. This is the cube in five-dimensional space, the cube of the expanding universe described in *Sefer Yetzirah*. According to tradition, the author of *Sefer Yetzirah* is Abraham, the first Jew, who pondered the nature of creation until, because of his sincerity and righteousness, the Creator revealed Himself to him. Originally, his name was Abram, whose numerical value is exactly 243. Upon commanding him to circumcise himself at the age of 99, God gave an additional *hei* to his name, converting it to Abraham, and bringing its numerical value to 248. The additional *hei*, which equals 5, is the secret of the five coordinates of five-dimensional space.

The human body possesses 248 limbs.[3] In the Torah, there are 248 positive commandments, whose purpose is to permeate the 248 human limbs with Divine consciousness. Of Abraham, it is said that even his heel knew God. Thus, God created man to reflect, in his body and soul, the five-dimensional hypercube of creation.

To understand the topology described above, let us examine the following chart:

dimensions of cube	0	1	2	3	4	5	6
points	1	2	4	8	16	32	64
lines	0	1	4	12	32	80	192
areas	0	0	1	6	24	80	240
volumes	0	0	0	1	8	40	160
4-dimensional-volumes	0	0	0	0	1	10	60
5-dimensional-volumes	0	0	0	0	0	1	12
6-dimensional-volumes	0	0	0	0	0	0	1
sum of components	1	3	9	27	81	243	729

Let us now rearrange the chart so that its diagonal lines appear horizontally:

---

3. *Ohalot* 1:8.

1	1	1	1	1	1	1
2	4	6	8	10	12	
4	12	24	40	60		
8	32	80	160			
16	80	240				
32	192					
64						

This arrangement can be understood by considering Pascal's triangle:

```
                        1
                     1     1
                  1     2     1
               1     3     3     1
            1     4     6     4     1
         1     5    10    10     5     1
      1     6    15    20    15     6     1
   1     7    21    35    35    21     7     1
1     8    28    56    70    56    28     8     1
```

In Pascal's triangle, the sums of the numbers appearing in each row are the powers of 2. The diagonal lines give "triangular numbers" in increasing dimensions.

(1 1 1 1 1... are the triangular numbers in 0 dimension, for a 0-dimensional triangle is a single point; 1 2 3 4 5... are the triangular numbers in 1 dimension, for a 1-dimensional triangle is a line; 1 3 6 10 15... are the triangular numbers in 2 dimensions, for the triangle of n is the sum of all numbers from 1 to n; 1 4 10 20 35... are the triangular numbers in 3 dimensions, for a 3-dimensional triangle is a tetrahedron, the sum of all 2-dimensional triangles from the triangle of 1 to the triangle of n. And so forth.)

Examining the derivative chart of the components of the cube in multi-dimensions, we now see that its rows are in fact the powers of 2 times the triangular numbers in increasing dimensions:

- 1 1 1 1 1 ... = 2^0 times the triangles in 0 dimension.
- 2 4 6 8 10 ... = 2^1 times the triangles in 1 dimension.
- 4 12 24 40 60 ... = 2^2 times the triangles in 2 dimensions.
- 8 32 80 160 ... = 2^3 times the triangles in 3 dimensions.
- 16 80 240 ... = 2^4 times the triangles in 4 dimensions.
- 32 192 ... = 2^5 times the triangles in 5 dimensions.
- 64 ... = 2^6 times the triangles in 6 dimensions.
- and so forth.

As noted, the sum of all of the components of a cube in n dimensions is 3^n. Thus, we may conclude that the essence of a "cube" in all dimensions is related to the number 3. To experience in our meditation of "Living in Divine Space" the essence of the cubic, expanding universe around us, we must attune our consciousness to the unity of the three basic dimensions of length, breadth, and height. These three dimensions define six extremities, corresponding to the six constant commandments of the Torah.

11

The Archetypal Souls of Israel[1]

The order of the *sefirot* is the order of the manifestation in the soul (and in the Divine creative process) of these spiritual archetypes, beginning with the forefathers of Israel. The order of the commandments is that of the rectification process of the soul, and thus, most appropriately, the order of our meditation. This is the order in which these commandments appear in the Torah, with the exception of the last commandment.

Similarly, the six archetypal souls evolve in chronological order with the exception of the last, Joseph, who, though existentially connected to his father, Jacob, and chronologically following him, fully manifests in the spiritual evolution of the collective soul of Israel only after Moses and Aaron. Even more precisely, Aaron was older than Moses; and so, the last three archetypal souls appearing here, corresponding to the triplet of *sefirot netzach-hod-yesod*, manifest, chronologically, in reverse order.

Thus chronologically, Moses, who appears last, corresponds to the first of the constant commandments of the Torah, the first of the Ten Commandments, "I am GOD, your God." This exemplifies the principle in Kabbalah that "The

---

1. See p. 24.

end is wedged in the beginning and the beginning in the end."[2] In a certain sense, all begins with eternity (*netzach*, the Divine attribute of Moses) and all concludes with eternity, thus creating an eternal cycle of Divine consciousness in the soul.

The chronological order of the six constant commandments of the Torah is thus:

1	to love God	Abraham
2	to fear God	Isaac
3	to unify God	Jacob
4	to guard one's mind from negative thoughts	Joseph
5	to deny the existence of other gods	Aaron
6	to believe in God and His Divine Providence	Moses

Clearly, to love God implies believing in Him. Abraham was indeed the first man to consummately believe in God.[3] But the faith that the Jewish soul acquires from its connection to the archetypal soul of Moses is greater than that which it inherits from Abraham. After witnessing the miracle of the splitting of the Red Sea, the Jewish people came to consummate faith in God and in His servant, Moses: "And they believed in GOD and in Moses His servant."[4] In Hassidism, it is explained that the initial level of belief in God, in His immanence, is that which we inherit from Abraham. The additional level of faith, in God's essential

---

2. *Sefer Yetzirah* 1:7.

3. Genesis 15:6.

4. Exodus 14:31.

transcendence, we acquire through our spiritual connection to Moses. From this we may understand why, chronologically, Abraham comes first and Moses last.

The homily of the archetypal souls building the walls of the Holy Temple, which appears in later rabbinic literature, is based on the teaching of the sages[5] that Abraham called the Temple a "mountain," Isaac called it a "field," and Jacob called it a "house." Each was referring to the Temple, God's house-to-be.

Numerically, the three words for "mountain" (*har* = 205), "field" (*sadeh* = 309), and "house" (*bayit* = 412) appear to be arranged in linear order (with the slight divergence that 309 is 104 more than 205, while 412 is 103 more than 309). We are further taught that Adam, who was created from the dust of the site of the altar of the Temple, sacrificed there an offering (*minchah* = 103). Finally, Moses offered 515 prayers. The very word for "prayer" [*tefilah*] equals 515, the identical value of the verb used in the Torah for Moses' prayer, "and I pleaded" [*va-etchanan*] to enter the Land of Israel and merit to build the Holy Temple.

Thus, we observe a linear progression from 103 to 2 times 103 (206, with the slight diversion of –1, 205), to 3 times 103 (309), to 4 times 103 (412), to 5 times 103 (515)! Each step of this progression adds a new dimension of consciousness with regard to the Temple. And so, we conclude that Adam built (on the spiritual plane) the west wall of the Temple, and so on.

---

5. *Pesachim* 88a.

God himself described the Temple as a house of prayer, as it is written, "My house shall be a house of prayer."[6]

The numerical value of the word for "prayer," *tefilah*, is 515, the fifth multiple of 103, as noted above. The word for "house," *bayit*, is 412, the fourth multiple of 103. Thus, the numerical value of the idiom, "house of prayer," *beit tefilah*, is 927, 9 times 103. Together, the levels of Jacob, who, by calling the Temple site *bayit*, built on the spiritual plane the eastern wall of the Temple (the fourth dimension of the spiritual Temple, represented by the number 412) and Moses, who, by offering 515 prayers to enter the Land of Israel and build the Holy Temple in Jerusalem, built on the spiritual plane the roof of the Temple (the fifth dimension of the spiritual Temple, represented by the number 515) join to give the inner content and purpose of the Temple, as stated in the verse mentioned above, "My house shall be a *house of prayer*." This is the level of King David.

King David brings down, i.e., actualizes, the 515 supplications of Moses to enter the Land of Israel, for David, the archetypal soul of *malchut*, is identified in essence with the Land of Israel, its special commandments, and its innermost heart—the Holy Temple in Jerusalem. King David devoted his life to preparing the materials for the Temple and planning all the details of its construction. God did not allow him to build it himself, but rather promised him that his son Solomon would realize his deepest desire to build the

---

6. Isaiah 56:7.

Temple. Because of David's dedication and self-sacrifice to build the Temple, the Temple is called David's house.[7]

---

7. 1 Kings 12:16.

12

The Hypercube[1]

We have discussed six of the ten *sefirot* (from *chesed* to *yesod*) as they correspond to the six sides of our cubic meditation/sanctuary, and the seventh (*malchut*) as it corresponds to its interior. The remaining three of the ten *sefirot*, *keter* ("crown"), *chochmah* ("wisdom"), and *binah* ("understanding"), also play a role in our meditation cube.

Since each of the six sides of our cubic sanctuary corresponds to one of the six constant commandments of the Torah, the very essence of our meditation is to link the dimension of time to the three dimensions of space (length, breadth, and height), thus producing a full, four-dimensional, space-time hypercube. In Kabbalah, we are taught that the two directions of the dimension of time, past and future, correspond to the two primary intellectual faculties of the soul, the two *sefirot* of *chochmah* ("wisdom") and *binah* ("understanding"), whose inner lights are *bitul* ("selflessness") and *simchah* ("joy"). These two are referred to allegorically as *Abba* ("father") and *Ima* ("mother") as they give birth to the six emotions of the heart, the six *sefirot* from *chesed* to *yesod*, which correspond to the six constant commandments of the Torah.

---

1. See p. 24

Chochmah and *binah* correspond, at a higher level than *netzach* and *hod*, to Moses and Aaron, who, as we have seen, also correspond to the first two of the Ten Commandments. Indeed, the Ten Commandments are articulated twice in the Torah,[2] alluding to the fact that they manifest at two levels of the soul: the consciousness of past and future in time (*chochmah* and *binah*) and the consciousness of *above* and *below* in space (*netzach* and *hod*).

The relation of time-consciousness to the first two of the Ten Commandments—more so than to the other of the constant commandments of the Torah—is that only here, in the verse from which the first commandment is derived, is there an explicit reference to a historical (time-oriented) event: "I am GOD, your God, who has taken you out of the land of Egypt, out of the house of bondage."

All of Jewish history, on the collective plane of the Jewish people as well as on the personal plane of every individual Jew in his or her lifetime, oscillates between exile and redemption; all exiles are referred to as "Egypt" and all redemptions are referred to as the Exodus from Egypt.

Thus, the consciousness of this commandment (and its complement, the second commandment)—the experience of God liberating us from Egypt, on both the spiritual and physical planes—carries us through time, continually reinforcing in our souls the conviction that God exists, here and now, and that no god exists besides Him.

_____

2. Exodus 20 and Deuteronomy 5.

In addition to the six constant commandments described here in our meditation, we are taught that in the future, with the coming of the Messiah and the building of the third, eternal Temple, the *mitzvah* of *teshuvah* (the commandment to return to God) and the *mitzvah* of *talmud Torah* (the commandment to study the Torah, gaining new insights in its understanding) will be continually manifest in the consciousness of the soul.

The *mitzvah* of *teshuvah* corresponds to the *sefirah* of *binah* and the soul-root of Aaron. Aaron was, in a certain sense, responsible for the sin of the Golden Calf, the most all-inclusive sin of Israel, for which he returned to God in complete *teshuvah*. The *mitzvah* of *talmud Torah* corresponds to the *sefirah* of *chochmah* and the soul-root of Moses, the giver of the Torah.

Indeed, these two commandments are included in the first two of the Ten Commandments, continual innovation in Torah in the first (new insight into the Torah is an experience of spiritual liberation), and continual *teshuvah* in the second (departing from dependency on any other force besides God, and thereby approaching and coming closer to Him).

To complete the picture, the supreme "crown" (*keter*), the first and highest of the *sefirot*, corresponding to the super-consciousness of the soul in general, is reflected in the *mitzvah* of *kiddush Hashem* (the commandment to be ever-ready to sacrifice one's life for God).[3] This state of consciousness will become constant at the time of the resurrection of the dead.

---

3. Leviticus 22:32.

In essence, the level of *keter*, as reflected in the *mitzvah* of *kiddush Hashem*, corresponds to the fifth dimension of Divine consciousness, above four-dimensional space-time. The meaning of *kiddush Hashem* being a constant commandment in the human psyche (soul in body) is that it unites, from another "place" altogether (the fifth dimension), with the four dimensions of space-time.

To summarize:

sefirah	constant *mitzvah*	in history	dimension
keter	*kiddush HaShem*	resurrection	fifth dimension—soul
chochmah	*talmud Torah*	Messianic era	fourth dimension—time
binah	*teshuvah*		
chesed	loving God	now	three dimensions—space length, breadth, height
gevurah	fearing God		
tiferet	unifying God		
netzach	belief in God		
hod	not serving idols		
yesod	guarding thought		
malchut	prayer	aspiring to be constant	middle point

13

The Six Remembrances[1]

At the end of our morning prayers, in accordance with
the version of Rabbi Yitzchak Luria, as arranged by Rabbi
Shneur Zalman of Liadi, we recite the "six remembrances,"
six things a Jew is to remember every day of his life.[2]

---

1. See p. 25.

2. The blessing before the recitation of the *Shema* in the morning ends: "…You
have chosen us from all nations and tongues, and in love, You have brought us
near, O our King, to Your great Name, that we may praise You and proclaim
Your Oneness and love Your Name. Blessed are You, GOD, who chooses His
people Israel with love."

Rabbi Shneur Zalman of Liadi writes in his *Shulchan Aruch* (*Orach Chaim* 60:4)
that "Remembering [our] standing at Mt. Sinai [to receive the Torah], the
episode of Amalek, the episode of Miriam, and the episode of the Golden Calf,
are positive commandments from the Torah. There are authorities who say that
it is also a commandment to remember Shabbat every day. It is proper to
remember these [concepts] in proximity to the recital of the *Shema*:

- when one says 'You have chosen us [from all nations and tongues]' one
  should remember the giving of the Torah and how 'You have brought us
  near' to Mt. Sinai;

- [when one says] 'to Your great Name,' [one should remember] the episode
  of Amalek, for God's Name is not complete until his seed will be wiped
  out;

- [when one says] 'to praise You' [one should remember that] the mouth was
  created only to praise [God] and not to utter slander—this is remembering
  the episode of Miriam;

Naturally, we would expect these six remembrances to correspond to the six constant commandments of the Torah.

In the order they are listed in the *siddur* (which is neither the order of their appearance in the Torah nor their chronological order), the six remembrances are:

- to remember the Exodus from Egypt,
- to remember the revelation of the Giving of the Torah at Mt. Sinai,
- to remember the war Amalek fought against the Jews after the Exodus,
- to remember how we provoked God's wrath in the desert,
- to remember how God struck Miriam with leprosy, and
- to remember the Sabbath.[3]

- [when one says, in the third paragraph of the *Shema*,] '...and remember all the commandments of GOD,' [one should think that] this refers to Shabbat, whose importance is equivalent to that of all the other commandments together;

- as for the episode of the Golden Calf, there are authorities who say that one should remember [this] when one says '...and proclaim Your Oneness in love,' i.e., not as when they made the Calf, and were not in love with the Holy One, blessed be He."

The third paragraph of the *Shema* also mentions that "I am GOD, your God, who brought you out of the land of Egypt." Thus, all six remembrances are mentioned in connection with the recitation of the *Shema* in the morning.

3. The six remembrances as phrased in the Torah are:

- "...So that you remember the day you came out of the Land of Egypt all the days of your life" (Deuteronomy 16:3).

- "But beware and guard your soul scrupulously, lest you forget the things that your eyes have seen, and lest they be removed from your heart all the days of your life; make known to your children and to your children's

First, let us note, with regard to the spiritual service of meditation, that a "remembrance" is a state of consciousness that remains in the wake of a life-experience or a meditative experience. In the terminology of Kabbalah and Hassidism, this is called "an impression" (*reshimu*). When unable to meditate in depth, we are taught at least to recall previous experiences of Divinity, to remember. Thus, in a certain sense, remembrance is the ideal state of continuous consciousness we are striving to attain here. When we begin in the morning with in-depth meditation, we hope to remember the impression of the meditation the entire day.

Often, in the attempt to establish one-to-one correspondences between parallel sets of concepts, several possibilities present themselves. This is due to the interrelationships between the concepts and the inter-inclusion of the concepts one in the other. We will here present the most straightforward one-to-one correspondence

children [what you saw] on the day when you stood before GOD, your God, at Horeb" (*ibid.* 4:9-10).

- "Remember what Amalek did to you on the way as you came out of Egypt; how he met you on the way, and cut down all the weak who straggled behind you, when you were weary and exhausted; and he did not fear God. Therefore, when GOD, your God, will relieve you of all your enemies around you, in the land which GOD, your God, gives you as a hereditary portion, you shall blot out the memory of Amalek from under heaven. Do not forget!" (*ibid.* 25:17-19).

- "Remember, do not forget, how you provoked GOD, your God, to wrath in the desert" (*ibid.* 9:7).

- "Remember what GOD, your God, did to Miriam on the way, as you came out of Egypt" (*ibid.* 24:9).

- "Remember the Shabbat day to sanctify it" (Exodus 20:8).

between the six constant commandments of the Torah and the six daily remembrances:

1. The remembrance of the Exodus, the epitome of which is on Passover night, conveys to the Jewish soul the impression of the love between God and Israel, a love symbolized in the Torah by that of groom and bride. In Kabbalah, Passover is the festival of love. On Passover, we read the Song of Songs, the song of love between the Divine groom and His bride. Of the Exodus, it is said: "I remember for you the kindness of your youth, the love of your espousals, how you followed Me into the desert, into an unsown land."[4] God remembers our kindness (*chesed*) and love (*ahavah*) for Him, and we remember His kindness and love for us. Thus, the remembrance of the Exodus corresponds to the constant commandment to love God, to the *right*.

2. The remembrance of God's revelation to us at Sinai is the revelation of *above*, as stated in the verse, "You have seen that from heaven I have spoken with you."[5] This clearly corresponds to the constant commandment to believe in God and His Providence. "The Torah was commanded to us by Moses,"[6] who corresponds to the *sefirah* of *netzach* and the direction of *above*. *Netzach* means "victory" or "eternity," and so is the Torah eternal, never to be replaced.

As we shall see, the essence of the first of the Ten Commandments, the Torah-source of this commandment, is

---

4. Jeremiah 2:2.

5. Exodus 20:19.

6. Deuteronomy 33:4.

expressed in its first words: "I am GOD, your God...," referring to the revelation of God's very essence. The verse continues: "...Who has taken you out of the land of Egypt, out of the house of bondage." The revelation of Sinai recalls the Exodus from Egypt. *Adult* belief in God's essence recalls the love of *youth* for Him.

3. The remembrance of Amalek corresponds to the *rear*, the constant commandment to shield one's mind from negative thoughts of heresy and lust, as expressed by the idiom used in the Torah to describe Amalek's attack on Israel, "how he met you on the way, and cut down [lit., 'tailed you,' the tail being a symbol of the rear] all the weak who straggled *behind* you." As we shall see, Amalek is the arch-enemy of Israel, who attacks from the rear. Based upon the numerical equivalence of *Amalek* (240) and "doubt" (*safek*, 240), the Ba'al Shem Tov teaches that Amalek is the source of heretical thoughts. Heretical thoughts themselves provoke thoughts of lust.[7]

4. The remembrance of the Sin of the Golden Calf most clearly corresponds to the constant commandment not to serve idols. Instead of relying solely upon God, the Provider of all our needs, the people placed their reliance in a graven image.

5. The remembrance of the punishment God meted out to Miriam corresponds to the constant commandment to fear God. Miriam, punished with leprosy, was ostracized from the camp of Israel, where God's Presence was manifest. When we see that even the most beloved to God are held

---

7. See Rashi *ad loc.* on the symbol of the "tail."

accountable for their deeds, and become (temporarily) severed from the revelation of His Presence, we come to fear being severed from God and we stand in awe of His Presence.[8]

6. Finally, the remembrance of the day of Shabbat corresponds to the constant commandment to believe in God's absolute unity, to know His infinite mercy over all. Shabbat is the revelation of "the higher unification," as expressed in the first verse of the *Shema*, "Hear, O Israel, GOD is our God; GOD is one." The final letters of the three words that precede this verse in the Torah, *zavat chalav udevash* ("flowing with milk and honey"), spell (backwards) *Shabbat*.

(The numerical value of the word *Shabbat* is 702. 702 = 27 times 26, which is the numerical value of the Name *Havayah*. This is the sum of all numbers from 1 to 26, that is, 351, and, in return, from 26 to 1, that is, 351, as explained in Kabbalah. Thus, Shabbat is understood to be the secret of the two appearances of the Name *Havayah* in the verse, "Hear, O Israel, GOD is our God, GOD is one." The full numerical value of the verse "Hear, O Israel..." is 1118 = 43 times 26. Together with the word *Shabbat*, 1118 ⊥ 702 = 1820 = exactly 70 times 26, the total number of appearances of the Name *Havayah* in the Five Books of Moses! 1820 is 10 times 182, the numerical value of the name of the third patriarch, Jacob, who corresponds to the *sefirah* of *tiferet*, the east or *front* side of our meditative cube.)

---

8. *Zevachim* 115b.

9. Deuteronomy 6:3.

The order of the remembrances as listed in the *Siddur* is thus from *chesed* to *netzach* to *yesod* to *hod* to *gevurah* to *tiferet* (whose inner soul is *da'at*, "the higher unification" expressed in the first verse of the *Shema*). This order, when superimposed on the sefirotic tree, forms a never-ending circle. The process of remembrance, the Divine impression manifest in the consciousness of the soul, is circular innature:

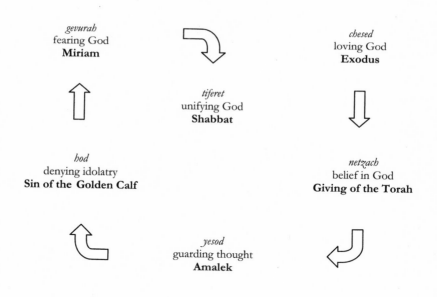

gevurah
fearing God
Miriam

tiferet
unifying God
Shabbat

chesed
loving God
Exodus

hod
denying idolatry
Sin of the Golden Calf

netzach
belief in God
Giving of the Torah

yesod
guarding thought
Amalek

In contrast, in-depth meditation is "straight":

sefirah	constant *mitzvah*	remembrance
chesed	loving God	Exodus from Egypt
gevurah	fearing God	Miriam
tiferet	unifying God	Shabbat
netzach	belief in God	Giving of the Torah
hod	denying idolatry	Sin of the Golden Calf
yesod	guarding thought	Amalek

14

Unity[1]

The first two of the Ten Commandments are the affirmation of our "faith in general" and its complement, the negation of the antithesis of that faith. In the commandment to unify God, the negation of its antithesis is part of—indeed, one and the same as—the thesis. In fact, the sages teach us that in the verse "Hear, O Israel, GOD is our God, GOD is one," "Hear, O Israel, GOD is our God" alludes to the first of the Ten Commandments, "I am GOD, your God...," whereas "GOD is one" alludes to the second of the Ten Commandments, "You shall have no other gods...."[2]

"Faith in particular" is articulated in our proclamation that "GOD is our God." This expresses the unification of God with the soul-root of Israel (as in the first Commandment, "I am GOD, *your* God, that has taken *you* out of the land of Egypt, out of the house of bondage"). In the terminology of the Ba'al Shem Tov (who identifies three general dimensions of reality: Worlds, Souls, and Divinity), this is the unification of Divinity and Souls. "GOD is one" is the unification of God with all of creation, the unification of Divinity and Worlds. In the terminology of the *Zohar*, these two unifications are referred to as "He and His life-force are

---

1. See p. 44.
2. *Y. Berachot* 1:5.

152

one [the unification of Divinity and Souls]; He and His limbs are one [the unification of Divinity and Worlds]."[3]

Rashi explains that "GOD is one" will only become fully manifest in the future, when all peoples will call upon the one God of Israel. Here, we see that "GOD is one" refers in particular to the negation of all forms of idolatry, i.e., those "shells" that hide the unification of Divinity and Worlds.

Thus, unifying God in our statement of faith—"GOD is one"—implies the negation of even the subtlest form of idol worship (such as becoming angry[4]). In "faith in particular"—"GOD is [absolutely] one"—the two aspects of affirmation and negation themselves manifest as one. (Ultimately, Worlds will elevate to the level of Souls, and Souls will become absolutely one with Divinity, as taught in Hassidism.)

The first *two* of the six constant commandments are *two* of the 613 commandments of the Torah. (According to Maimonides' order of enumerating the commandments, these are the *first* two.) With regard to the commandment to unify God, *one* of the 613, a constant duty of the heart, we are commanded to recite the verse, "Hear, O Israel…" *twice* a day, morning and evening. These *two* times of recital every day reflect the *two* aspects of affirmation and negation that are inherently *one* in this commandment.

---

3. See *Tikunei Zohar*, introduction (3b).

4. See p. 45.

15

Frontal Consciousness[1]

The first and last letters (*shin-dalet*) of the verse, "Hear, O Israel, GOD is our God; GOD is One" (***Sh**ema Israel Havayah Elokeinu, Havayah Echa**d***) are the same as those of the phrase from Psalms, "I place GOD in front of me always" (***Sh**iviti Havayah lenegdi tam**id***).[2] These two verses, which complement one another, are the two fundamental expressions of frontal Divine consciousness in the Bible. The subtle difference between the two lies in the fact that the first, the words spoken by Moses to the generation about to enter and conquer the Land of Israel,[3] expresses only the recognition of GOD our God (the God of the collective soul of Israel) as being absolutely one. In the second verse, the words of King David in Psalms (which give expression to the deepest heartfelt supplication of each and every individual soul to God), there appears a definite, individual subject—"*I* place GOD in front of *me* always." *I* experience God in every facet of *my* life. (We will see that these two verses, from the Torah and from Psalms, correspond to right-frontal consciousness and left-frontal consciousness, respectively.)

---

1. See p. 46

2. Psalms 16:8.

3. In *Tanya*, ch. 25, it is stated that in order to enter, conquer, and live in Israel, it is necessary to have the dedication and self-sacrifice implied in "Hear O Israel..." in the *front* of one's consciousness at all times.

These two letters (*shin-dalet*) spell *shad*, meaning "breast," located in the front of the body. In the Talmud we find that King David praised God for having created his mother's breasts in the front of her body, "in the place of understanding [i.e., the place of 'the understanding heart']."[4]

The value of *shad* is 304. When the two breasts are considered together, 2 times 304 equals 608, which equals 32 (the value of *lev* ["heart"]) times 19 (the value of *Chava* [Eve]) giving us the "heart of Eve," who was "the mother of all life."

Thus, these two verses are the two spiritual breasts that nurse the frontal consciousness of the Jewish soul, raising it to maturity, so that it can experience the one God of Israel, Creator of the universe, in *front* at all times.

The verse in the Torah—"Hear O Israel, GOD is our God, GOD is one"—corresponds, in particular, to the right spiritual breast of Divine consciousness, whereas the verse in Psalms—"I place GOD in front of me always"—corresponds, in particular, to the left spiritual breast of Divine consciousness. In general, the relation between Torah (study) and prayer (Psalms) is that of right to left. The light of the Torah is descending light, similar to the nature of water to descend, as we see from the statement in the Talmud that the Torah is likened to water, "There is no water but the Torah."[5] Descending light characterizes the right axis of the supernal *sefirot*. Heartfelt prayer (and reciting Psalms) gives expression to the soul's fiery love, a light ascending to God. "Prayer is in

---

4. *Berachot* 10a.

5. *Bava Kama* 17a.

the place of sacrifice,"[6] thus our heartfelt prayers are like the fiery sacrificial offerings of the Temple, which are called "the Divine fires."[7] Ascending light characterizes the left axis of the *sefirot*.

In Kabbalah, we learn that in the time of Moses there were two prophets who prophesied in the camp of Israel— Eldad and Meidad—who correspond, mystically, to the two breasts of the collective soul of Israel. Both of their names conclude with the syllable *dad*, which, similar to *shad*, means "breast." Eldad is seen in Kabbalah to correspond to the right breast and Meidad to the left breast. The numerical value of *Eldad* is 39, which equals "GOD is one" (*HaShem echad*), the conclusion of the first verse of frontal consciousness, "Hear O Israel...," which corresponds to the right breast, as stated above. The numerical value of *Meidad* is 58, which equals the word for "grace" (*chen*), the grace that we find in the eyes of God when we place Him in the *front* of our consciousness always. 58 equals, as well, "GOD is the only one" (*HaShem yachid*), a level of consciousness even higher than that of "GOD is one."

The origin of the left is always higher than the origin of the right. The individual consciousness of the left, explained above, rises in its ultimate source to a level of consciousness where either we exist as an integral part, as it were, of the one absolutely single God or we do not exist at all. On the other hand, the collective consciousness of "GOD is our God, GOD

6. *Berachot* 26b.

7. Leviticus 4:35, etc.

is one" implies that God is one in the souls of Israel, His children, and in all of His creation.

Together, *Eldad* and *Meidad*, 39 and 58, equal 97, the value of *Mehitabel*, the name of the woman who represents, in Kabbalah, the rectification of Divine consciousness. Mehitabel was the wife of Hadar, the eighth king of Edom, who, in Kabbalah, symbolizes the beginning of the rectification of consciousness. (The previous seven kings of Edom symbolize the primordial "breaking of the vessels," the breakdown of Divine consciousness.) In the narrative of the Torah, the first seven kings "reign and die," while the last king, Hadar, and his wife, Mehitabel, "reign" but do not die.

(97 is the 26th prime number, beginning with 1. A prime number is indivisible, and thus alludes to God's essential, indivisible unity. From 1 to 100 there are 26 prime numbers, 26 "ones." 26 is the value of God's essential Name, *Havayah*. 26 = 13 plus 13. There are 13 primes from 1 to 37 and another 13 to 100. 101 is the 27th prime number. From 1 to 1000 there are 169 = 13 times 13 prime numbers, 997 being the 169th prime.)

97 is also the combined value of God's two mystical Names, whose numerical values are 45 and 52, the Name of 45 representing the right-frontal consciousness of "GOD is one," and the Name of 52 representing the left-frontal consciousness of "placing GOD in front of me always." In every "point" of rectified consciousness these two Names must unite, as is taught in Kabbalah.

The continuation of the verse in Psalms, "I place GOD in front of me always," reads: "...for as He is at my right hand, I shall not falter." Here, then, *"front*-consciousness" is juxtaposed with and leads to *"right*-consciousness." From the consciousness of "Hear, O Israel..." we come to the consciousness of the next commandment, the following verse in the Torah, "And you shall love GOD...," as will be explained. This itself implies that our consciousness of God's absolute oneness is to be equated with our consciousness of God's absolute goodness, for love is aroused toward the one who is good.

The fact that both facets of faith—"faith in general" (*above*) and "faith in particular" (in *front*)—lead to love, indicates that there are also two facets of love: love in general (loving God because He is the supreme, omnipotent Redeemer) and love in particular (loving God because He, the absolute one, is the absolute good, as reflected in each and every of His deeds).

Loving people "in general" does not necessarily mean loving everything about them; loving people "in particular" means not only loving everything about them but also loving all others whom they love. With respect to God, this means loving every Jew, because God loves every Jew, as it is said, "I love you, says GOD."[8]

Loving God in general entails the conviction that "all that God does is for the good,"[9] whether we see it or not. Loving God in particular implies that in every act of Divine Providence (even an act which for others would appear negative), we actually see that "this, too, is for the good."[10]

---

8. Malachi 1:2; see *HaYom Yom*, 28 *Nisan*.

9. *Berachot* 60b.

10. *Ta'anit* 21a.

The Ba'al Shem Tov teaches that the verse, "I place GOD in front of me always" can be read: "All things are equal to me when I am conscious of God."[11] When we remember that all things come from God, and are therefore *ipso facto* absolutely good, all things become equal to us, as the Ba'al Shem Tov says, "whether others praise him or embarrass him...it is all the same."[12] In this verse, we see explicitly that an awareness of God's unity should always be in the forefront of our consciousness.

"I place GOD in front of me always" implies the duty to observe all six constant commandments.[13] From this we understand that the all-inclusive Jewish consciousness is the frontal consciousness of "Hear, O Israel...," which is the verse in the Torah mirrored by the verse in Psalms "I place GOD in front of me always."

---

11. *Tzava'at HaRibash* 2 (ed. *Kehot*).

12. *Ibid.*

13. *Biur Halachah*, quoted above.

16

Emulating Divine Mercy[1]

As we saw above, the power to redeem from exile is associated with the belief in God, the direction of *above* in our meditation. Thus, the desire to redeem, a desire that springs from feelings of mercy, relates the frontal consciousness to the *above* consciousness. From feelings of great mercy we are motivated to emulate God, the Redeemer of Israel. Although we cannot truly emulate His omnipotence (the essence of the recognition of Divinity implicit in the first commandment), in recognition of God's absolute unity we can and should become aroused in great mercy to redeem Godly sparks imprisoned in the shackles of spiritual exile.

Indeed, the greatest cause for arousing mercy on another soul (or on our own soul) is that we do not possess in our consciousness the Divine truth of God's absolute unity and mercy on all, a truth that, when integrated in our mind and heart, serves to sweeten all of the bitterness of life.

On the verse "...and you shall walk in His ways,"[2] the sages comment: "Just as He is merciful, so shall you be merciful; just as He is...."[3] The first commandment—to believe in God and to sense that now, having been redeemed

---

1. See p. 48.

2. Deuteronomy 28:9.

3. *Shabbat* 133b, *Y. Peah* 1, *Sotah* 14a, *Tana d'vei Eliahu Rabbah* 26.

from the confines of Egypt, we are free to ascend toward God—entails the aspiration to emulate God in general, whereas the commandment to unify God entails emulating Him in particular, emulating His Divine attributes.

Of all the attributes here enumerated, mercy is listed first. Furthermore, mercy is one of the fundamental, intrinsic characteristics of the Jew—the other two being modesty and generosity.[4]

The Hebrew word *Israel* is in fact read in Hassidism as an acronym for the phrase "May God Almighty bestow mercy upon you" (*V'Kel Shakai yiten lachem rachamim*), which can also be read as: "May God Almighty give you [the attribute of] mercy."[5]

The sages state that, "One who acts with mercy upon [God's] creatures is acted upon with mercy from heaven."[6] In the Torah we find that "[God] will give you [the attribute of] mercy [on others] and [in turn, because of your mercy on others] will have mercy on you."[7] The two readings of "May God Almighty bestow mercy upon you" are thus seen to be inter-dependant.

The root of the word for "mercy," *rachamim*, is *rechem*, which means "womb." Above, we saw that frontal

---

4. *Yevamot* 79a, etc.; in most of the sources where these qualities are enumerated, mercy is listed first.

5. Genesis 43:14; *Likutei Moharan* 2:62; *cf.* footnote 31 in the introduction to *Shechinah Beineihem* (p. 53).

6. *Shabbat* 151b; *Pesikta Rabati* 39.

7. Deuteronomy 13:18.

consciousness relates to the experience of the two spiritual breasts of the collective Jewish soul, the two soul-roots of the prophets Eldad and Meidad (the numerical values of whose names, 39 and 58, equal "GOD is one," *HaShem echad*, and "GOD is the only one," *HaShem yachid*, respectively). The spiritual result of our frontal meditation is to create in our souls the fertile spiritual womb that will give birth to the Divine attribute of mercy, *rachamim*, so that we truly emulate God in all of His ways. This is indeed a messianic birth process, as it is said in reference to the Messiah, "you are My son, today I have given birth to you."[8] Every day (twice a day, evening and morning, when we recite the *Shema*) we give birth to the latent spark of the Messiah in our souls by bearing from our spiritual womb, in our frontal meditation, the Divine attribute of mercy. Of the Messiah it is said, "for he who has mercy on them [the people of Israel] will lead them."[9]

Thus, we see that frontal consciousness—meditating on God's oneness and singleness and fertilizing our souls to give birth to the Divine attribute of mercy—relates in particular to the consciousness of the female side of the collective soul of Israel. This is so for the *front* corresponds to the *sefirah* of *tiferet*, "beauty," the attribute most characteristic of woman, as in the phrase "the beauty of man"[10] (*tiferet adam*), which means woman.[11]

---

8. Psalms 2:7.

9. Isaiah 49:10.

10. *Ibid.* 44:13.

11. *Targum Yonatan ad loc.*

17

Fear[1]

Maimonides derives the commandment to fear God from the verse: "Fear GOD, your God."[2]

The numerical value of the verse from which Maimonides derives the commandment to love God, "And you shall love GOD, your God, with all your heart and with all your soul and with all your might," is 1644. When this is added to the numerical value of "Fear GOD, your God," 1104, the result is 2748 = 12 times 229. The number 12 is the numerical value of the word for "this is" (*zeh*, 12). The number 229 is the numerical value of the sum of "love" (*ahavah*, 13) and "fear" (*yirah*, 216). Thus, the sum of the numerical values of the Torah sources for the two commandments to love and to fear God equals "this is" times "love" plus "fear."

As we have seen, fearing God is actually a part of loving Him. This is alluded to in the verse quoted by Maimonides, which begins with the word *et*, an article which has no English equivalent.

(The word *et* is composed of two letters, *alef* and *tav*, the first and the last letters of the Hebrew alphabet,

---

1. See p. 59.

2. Deuteronomy 10:20.

respectively. Both the beginning and the end of Divine service is fear, as it is written: "The beginning of wisdom is the fear of GOD"[3] and "The final word, all having been understood, fear God and observe His commandments, for this is all [i.e., the ultimate life purpose] of man."[4]

The letter *alef*, the first letter of the alphabet, refers in particular to wisdom, *chochmah*, as explicitly stated in the verse, "I will teach you [*a'alefcha*, from the root *alef*] wisdom."[5] This is also indicated by the fact that creation begins with *et*: "In the beginning God created *et* [the heavens...]."[6] In the *Targum Yerushalmi*, "In the beginning" is translated as "With wisdom."

The letter *tav*, the last letter of the alphabet, refers in particular to understanding, *binah*, which, in Kabbalah, is referred to as the World to Come or "the end of days." In *Sefer Yetzirah*,[7] *chochmah* and *binah* are known as the "absolute [literally, 'depth of'] beginning" and the "absolute end," respectively. When the numerical values of *chochmah*, 73, and *binah*, 67, are added to that of *et*, 401, the result is 541, the numerical value of *Israel*. Israel is also regarded as the beginning and end of creation, for God created this world for the sake of Israel, in order that Israel inherit the World to Come: "The end of action is the beginning of thought."[8])

---

3. Psalms 111:10.

4. Ecclesiastes 12:13.

5. Job 33:33.

6. Genesis 1:1.

7. 1:5.

8. Liturgy, *Lechah Dodi*.

In the verse from which we derive the commandment to love God, the second word, following the command "And you shall love" (*veahavta*) is *et.* The sages teach that this word always implies something additional, though subordinate, implicit though not explicit in the text. In our case, the *et* following "And you shall love" implies that together with the love of God we must also possess the fear of God, from which we infer, as stated above, that fearing God is an integral part of loving God. This interpretation is greatly strengthened by the fact that the commandment to fear God itself begins with the word *et.*

On the other hand, "and now, O Israel...but to fear," the verse chosen here for our meditation on the commandment to fear God, implies that although, in a certain sense, fear is included within love, in another sense (and as explained above, regarding the *alef* of *et*), fear is "the beginning of Divine service, its foundation and its root."[9]

By first integrating the fear of God into our consciousness, we come to love God, to serve Him with all our heart and soul, and to observe all of God's commandments, as the verse continues, "...and now, O Israel, what does GOD ask of you, but to fear GOD, your God, to walk in all His ways, and to love Him, and to serve GOD, your God with all your heart and with all your soul, to keep the commandments of GOD and His statutes...." The sages[10] take note that God asks here for *one* thing—to fear Him—but then goes on to ask for a whole series of things,

9. *Tanya*, ch. 41.
10. *Yalkut Shimoni, Tehilim* 706.

virtually for everything! The implication is clear: from the one, initial point of fear, we come to serve God in every way.

As noted earlier, in general, fear precedes love in our service of God, as we find in the injunction to "Turn away from evil [fear] and do good [love]."[11] (Only exceptionally does love precede fear.[12]) Fear is the emotion that motivates turning from evil (observing the 365 prohibitive commandments of the Torah), whereas love is the emotion that motivates doing good (performing the 248 positive commandments of the Torah), as stated above.

An additional allusion pointing to fear as the beginning of Divine service is found in the verse: "His left hand is under my head." The word for "head" in Hebrew (*rosh*) means "beginning." Thus, "under my head" implies "supports my beginning," the beginning point being symbolized by the left hand, the emotion of fear. The level of fear that is the beginning of our service of God is "the lower fear," "the fear of sin," the fear that sin will sever our connection to God.

Of this level of fear, it is said: "all is in the hands of heaven except the fear of heaven."[13] "The fear of heaven" is thus understood to be the starting point and indeed the very essence of human free will.

---

11. Psalms 34:15; 37:27.

12. See *Tanya*, end of ch. 43 (62b).

13. *Berachot* 33b.

The sages further teach that God created the heavens with His right hand and the earth with His left.[14] From this, we may conclude that "all is in the hands of heaven" refers, in particular, to God's right hand (alluding to our service of love of God, to the *right*, a gift of heaven[15]), whereas "except the fear of heaven," which was given over to the hands of earthly humanity, refers, in particular, to our Divine service of the left hand, fear of heaven. And so we read in Psalms, "The heavens are the heavens of GOD, but the earth He has given to man."[16]

For this reason, the order of putting on *tefilin* is that we first put *tefilin* on the left arm, to imbue our hearts (the left arm is near the heart, which is situated on the left side of the body) with "the fear of heaven." The head *tefilin* then descends, as it were, from heaven (as indicated by the fact that according to many opinions in *halachah* we do not make a blessing over the head *tefilin*), enabling us to meditate on God's unity—"Hear O Israel, GOD is our God, GOD is one"—which in turn leads us to love Him in our hearts, as the verse continues, "And you shall love GOD, your God, with all your heart and with all your soul and with all your might."

14. *Pirkei d'Rabbi Eliezer* 19.

15. See *Tanya*, ch. 43.

16. Psalms 115:16.

18

The Inverted Seal[1]

We have seen that whereas the revelation of love is a product of intellect (that is, our contemplation of the oneness and greatness of God), fear inspires us to reach new horizons of intellect. In this sense, fear is more the "mindful" emotion and love the more "heartful."

This is an instance of the well-known Kabbalistic principle that "the lower phenomenon has the higher origin." Love, corresponding to the *sefirah* of *chesed*, is "higher" than fear, which, corresponding to the *sefirah* of *gevurah*, follows *chesed* in the order of the emotions of the heart. All emotions are rooted in the intellect, but since *gevurah* is lower, it reflects its root more than does *chesed*, and therefore fear contains more innate intellect than does love.

Carrying this principle one step further, mercy, corresponding to *tiferet*, the next of the *sefirot* of the heart, reflects an even higher root in the soul than does fear (that higher root is the super-conscious *keter*). The mercy of the heart reflects the "thirteen attributes of mercy" located in *keter*.

The principle that a lower phenomenon is rooted in a higher source is known, in Kabbalah and Hassidism, as "the

---

1. See p. 60.

inverted seal." In our case: the love of *chesed* is rooted in the "great love" (*ahavah rabah*) of *binah*; the fear of *gevurah* is rooted in the "shamefaced fear" of *chochmah*; the mercy of *tiferet* is rooted in the thirteen principles of Divine mercy of *keter*.

In Kabbalah, we are taught that with regard to the three primary attributes of the heart—*chesed* to the right, *gevurah* to the left, and *tiferet* in the middle—the mercy of *tiferet* (by virtue of its being in the middle) serves to connect the love of *chesed* to the fear of *gevurah*. Similarly, the thirteen attributes of mercy in *keter* (the origin of the middle axis of the sefirotic tree) unify the origin of fear in *chochmah* (situated at the top of the right axis) with the origin of love in *binah* (situated at the top of the left axis).

As noted above, the word for mercy, *rachamim*, derives from *rechem*, womb. The mercy of *keter* gives birth to (i.e., reveals) the latent potential inherent in *chochmah* and *binah*, known as "father" and "mother" in Kabbalah (preparing *chochmah* and *binah* to subsequently give birth to emotions of the heart). *Chochmah* and *binah* correspond to the first two letters of God's essential Name, *Havayah*, the *yud* and the *hei*. Their latent potential is revealed by the letters with which each of these two letters are "filled" when written in full: the *vav* and the *dalet* concealed within the *yud* (יוד) and the *yud* concealed within the *hei* (הי).[2]

---

2. At the level of *binah*, the letter *hei* is written with a *yud*, whereas at the level of the attributes of the heart, it is written with an *alef*, and at the level of *malchut*, it is written with a second *hei*. The name of the letter *yud* has only one spelling: *yud vav dalet*.

Now it becomes manifest that each of the two letters possesses the other in potential: Envisioning the *vav* of the *yud* entering into the *dalet* of the *yud* it becomes a *hei*; the *hei* is explicitly filled with a *yud*.

The *yud*, the initial point of the revelation of new insight, represents the higher state of fear in the soul, of which it is said, "The beginning of wisdom is the fear of GOD" (as cited earlier). To experience fear, especially the higher fear identified with *chochmah*, is to experience a piercing sensation of awe.

At the beginning of our discussion of the nature of Jewish meditation, we introduced the concept of "point, line, area." With regard to the emotions of the soul, fear is the point and love expands the point into a line and finally a full area (which, as explained earlier, includes higher dimensions as well). Love acts upon fear, adding dimensions of reality and tangibility to the zero-dimensional point, just as *binah*, the mother, acts upon *chochmah*, the father, developing its seminal, point-like essence into a multi-dimensional intellectual structure. (This process begins from the level of *binah* included within *chochmah*, of which it is said in *Sefer Yetzirah*,[3] "understand in wisdom.")

The three letters that compose the full spelling of the *yud* (*yud*, *vav*, and *dalet*) progress from a zero-dimensional point (the form of the letter *yud*), to a one-dimensional line (the form of the letter *vav*), to a two-dimensional area (the form of the letter *dalet*—two lines at right angle, representing the coordinates of two-dimensional space).

---

3. 1:4.

The form of the letter *hei* represents the ultimate area (or even volume, for it is explained in Kabbalah that the small, left leg of the *hei*, not touching its upper line, represents a third dimension, a coordinate running through the parchment upon which the *hei* is written). Thus, the *hei* of *binah* represents the ultimate state of development of the higher, all-encompassing "great love." The *yud* that fills the *hei* represents the inter-inclusion of the higher fear within the higher love (in the words of *Sefer Yetzirah*, "be wise in understanding").

And so we see that when the two letters are written in full, first the *yud* and then the *hei* (יוד הי), fear (represented by the *yud*) is at the beginning and fear is at the end (as mentioned above), with three stages of the development of love in the middle:

The one-dimensional line of the *vav* represents the arousal of love, the desire to extend oneself to another soul— to project oneself out of oneself in order to give—which follows the initial experience of fear, an experience that "freezes" one in place, as a point. The two-dimensional area of the *dalet* represents the augmented experience of love that comes with a sensitivity to the soul of the other and to his or her true needs. The *hei* is the experience of consummate love that comes with the union of the giver and the receiver, the joy (the essential inner experience of *binah*) of one's gift having been appropriate and well-received by the other.

		׳	*yud*	higher fear
׳	*yud*	ו	*vav*	arousal of love; desire to extend and give
		ד	*dalet*	experience of love in sensitivity to an other
ה	*hei*	ה	*hei*	consummate love; joy in the other receiving one's gift
		׳	*yud*	inter-inclusion of higher fear within higher love

When the two fully-spelled letters are "intertwined," the initial, root letter of the *yud* followed by the initial, root letter of the *hei*, then the latent potential within the *yud*, the *vav* and the *dalet*, and then the latent potential within the *hei*, the *yud*, we have יהודי (*yehudi*), "Jew." This is the ultimate secret of every Jewish soul, the power of the thirteen principles of mercy of *keter* to manifest and unify the source of fear in *chochmah* with the source of love in *binah*, each inter-included in the other. Kabbalah teaches that with the intention in our heart to "fear and love and love and fear" (the order here depicted), we stand before God and come to perform the commandments of the Torah, which link us (consciously, when our intention is correct, or unconsciously, when not) to God, the Giver of the Torah.

19

Being on Guard[1]

The last of the six constant commandments of the Torah is to always be on guard. In particular, we are to guard our minds from the intrusion of foreign thoughts. In general, though, the consciousness of being on guard keeps our attention concentrated on all of those thoughts that we are to keep in mind, all of the constant commandments of the Torah.

This commandment corresponds to the *sefirah* of *yesod*, whose power is "to guard the covenant" (*shemirat habrit*). In Kabbalah, the *sefirah* of *yesod* "summarizes" the experiences of the preceding five *sefirot*, the emotions of the heart, for which reason it is referred to as "all" (*kol*) in the verse, "To You, O GOD, is the *gedulah* ['greatness,' a synonym for *chesed*], and the *gevurah*, and the *tiferet*, and the *netzach*, and the *hod*, for all [*ki kol* = 80 = *yesod*] is in the heavens and the earth."[2] The numerical value of *kol* is 50 or 10 times 5 (manifesting all of the ten *sefirot* as reflected in each of the previous 5). And so, as said, this commandment serves to help one concentrate on all the preceding commandments.

---

1. See p. 67.
2. 1 Chronicles 29:11.

One of the 613 commandments of the Torah is to guard the Temple (*shemirat haMikdash*).[3] Here, in our meditation, by guarding our mind from foreign, negative thoughts, we guard our spiritual sanctuary or Temple, our Divine Space.

Today, our presence at the Western Wall of the Temple Mount commemorates the commandment to guard the Temple. By Divine Providence, this occurs on the west, the direction of the commandment to guard our mind from all impurity.

The wall is commonly referred to as "the Wailing Wall"; many tears have been shed there due to the "blemish of the covenant," in supplication to God to re-establish the covenant between Himself and Israel with the coming of the Messiah and the final redemption.

The Lubavitcher Rebbe explained[4] that upon the building of the third Temple, the first commandment to be performed will be "guarding the Temple." So, in our spiritual meditation and service, we may infer that this last of the six constant commandments is in a sense the first. In order to begin thinking positively, we must stop thinking negatively. Even if we are unable to consummately stop thinking negatively before entering the meditation of "Living in Divine Space," this should not deter us from meditating. The meditation itself will serve to push away negative thoughts by replacing them with good ones. Nevertheless, from the outset

---

3. *Mishneh Torah, Beit HaBechirah* 8:1.

4. Address of Shabbat *parashat Shemini*, 5750.

of meditation, we must intend to clean our minds from all foreign, impure matter, beseeching God for help in doing so.

20

An Allusion to the
Six Constant Commandments[1]

There is only *one* verse in the Torah that speaks of six
levels of Divine service:

אחרי ה' אלהיכם תלכו ואתו תיראו ואת מצותיו תשמרו
ובקלו תשמעו ואתו תעבדו ובו תדבקון.

You shall walk *after* GOD, *your God,*
and you shall fear *Him,*
and you shall observe *His commandments,*
and you shall listen *to His voice,*
and you shall serve *Him,*
and you shall cleave *to Him.*[2]

"Walking *after* GOD" alludes to the sixth constant
commandment of the Torah, as we have explained.

"Fearing God" explicitly refers to the constant
commandment to fear Him.

"Observing His commandments" refers to the
constant commandment to love Him, for, as we have

---

1. See p. 69.
2. Deuteronomy 13:5.

explained, love is the emotion that motivates the performance of all the positive commandments of the Torah.

"Listening to His voice" alludes to the experience of the Receiving of the Torah, in particular to the first of the Ten Commandments, of which it is said that we heard His voice speaking "I am GOD, your God..." from the heavens and all the directions of space.

"Serving Him" alludes to the second of the Ten Commandments, which requires of us commitment to serve God alone. In *Sefer Yetzirah*,[3] "service" is identified with the *sefirah* of *hod*, the direction of *below*.

"Cleaving to Him" refers to the constant commandment of unifying God. As in the marriage of man and woman, to "cleave" is to "become one" ("And he shall cleave to his wife, and they shall become one flesh"[4]).

To summarize:

"You shall *walk* after GOD, your God..."	guarding thought
"...and you shall *fear* Him..."	fearing God
"...and you shall *observe* His commandments..."	loving God
"...and you shall *listen* to His voice..."	believing in God
"...and you shall *serve* Him..."	denying idolatry
"...and you shall *cleave* to Him."	unifying God

---

3. 4:3.

4. Genesis 2:24.

21

"All Sevenths are Beloved"[1]

"All sevenths are beloved."[2] In relation to the six extremities of space, the "seventh" inner point or space of the cube is referred to in Kabbalah as "the holy chamber within."

Paralleling the days of the week, the six constant commandments of the Torah correspond to the six weekdays, while the seventh commandment of prayer corresponds to Shabbat, the day of rest. The six are relatively male while the seventh is female. Indeed, it is the seventh, the female, that arouses the six, the male.

As prayer strives to be constant it arouses us to retain awareness at all times of the six constant commandments of the Torah. We thus come to observe these commandments in the merit of prayer, the beloved seventh. In Kabbalah, this power of prayer is known as "arousal from below." Indeed, the very essence of our prayer should first and foremost be that we fulfill the six constant commandments of the Torah, to live together with God in Divine space-time. Prayer both fills the space of our meditative cube and gives it the conscious sense of time.

---

1. See p. 73.

2. *Vayikra Rabbah* 29:11.

The numerical value of the idiom for "the holy chamber," *heichal hakodesh*, 474, is that of the word for "knowledge," *da'at*. The six relatively male states of consciousness of the six constant commandments correspond to the six emotions of the heart, the six *sefirot* from *chesed* to *yesod*. The seventh, relatively female commandment of prayer corresponds to the *sefirah* of *malchut*, kingdom (whose archetypal soul is King David). When *malchut* fills the space created by the six parameters of *chesed* to *yesod* (the six directions of *above, below, front, back, right,* and *left,* which according to the orientation of the Torah are above, below, east, west, south, and north, respectively) it draws into the space Divine consciousness, i.e., *da'at*.

In Proverbs, we find that after one has built one's house (with wisdom and understanding) then, "with *da'at* are its rooms filled."[3] *Da'at*, Divine consciousness, fills the space that we have created by our meditative intention (employing our wisdom and understanding) to fulfill the six constant commandments of the Torah.

In the Torah,[4] *da'at* refers to the marital union of husband and wife, a union ideally identified with the sanctity of the seventh day, Shabbat. On Shabbat, *malchut* (the wife) arouses the six attributes of the heart (the husband) to unite with it in holy matrimony, by the power of *da'at*. For this reason, *heichal hakodesh* equals *da'at*.

The numerical difference between *malchut* (496) and *da'at* (*heichal hakodesh*, 474) is 22, the number of letters in the

---

3. Proverbs 24:4.
4. Genesis 4:1.

Hebrew alphabet. In Kabbalah, we are taught that the 22 letters originate in the "firmament" of *da'at*.[5] The 22 Hebrew letters are the vessels that contain and reveal Divine consciousness in our souls. The 22 letters are fully revealed in the *sefirah* of *malchut*, where they manifest their creative power. It is with these letters, at the level of *malchut*, that God created the world.

Thus, as explained above, in our meditation we focus on the holy letters that compose the verses from which the constant commandments of the Torah are derived. By focusing on what appear to be "inanimate" letters ("stones," in the idiom of *Sefer Yetzirah*[6]), we use them to draw *da'at*—Divine light and life-force—into our consciousness; indeed, they are perfectly designed for this. The fact that *Sefer Yetzirah* refers to letters as "stones" clearly indicates that they initially exist in our consciousness at the level of *malchut*, for *malchut* is the level of the inanimate in Kabbalah, possessing no life-force of its own, only that which it receives from the levels above it.

When added together, the numerical value of *heichal hakodesh* (474) and the six directions of Divine space, the parameters of the consciousness of the *heichal hakodesh*—*above* (*ma'alah*, 145), *below* (*matah*, 54), *east* (*mizrach*, 255), *west* (*ma'arav*, 312), *south* (*darom*, 250), *north* (*tzafon*, 226)—is 1716, or 26 times 66. 26 is the value of God's essential Name, *Havayah*. 66 is the value of "your God" (*Elokechah*). Thus, the

---

5. See *Tanya, Sha'ar HaYichud VehaEmunah* 5 [80a], quoting *Zohar* 2:209-210 and *Eitz Chaim* 44:3.

6. 4:16.

complete Divine consciousness of our meditation is "GOD, your God," as in the verse, "And you shall love GOD, your God, with all your heart and with all your soul and with all your might."

The value of the six directions themselves is 1242 or 6 times 207. 207 is thus the average value of the six directions. 207 equals "light" (*or*) and "infinity" (*ein sof*). Having attained total awareness of all six parameters of Divine space, one's consciousness becomes permeated with infinite Divine light.

The numerical value of the complete phrase, *heichal hakodesh be'emtza* ("the holy chamber within") is 677. To understand the significance of this number, we must introduce a fundamental teaching of the Arizal regarding the creative process in general.[7] Creation begins with light, "Let there be light." The initial revelation of light (*or*) must be followed by two additional stages, "water" (*mayim*) and "firmament" (*rakia*). On the first day of creation, the word "light" is mentioned five times[8] (corresponding to the Five Books of Moses[9]—"the Torah is light"[10]). On the second day of creation, the words "water" and "firmament" are each mentioned five times.[11] The Arizal explains that all of creation takes place by the initial light condensing to become water and finally to become firm, as a firmament. This process

---

7. *Eitz Chaim* 11:6 [2nd version], *et al.*

8. Genesis 1:3 (twice), 1:4 (twice), 1:5.

9. *Bereishit Rabbah* 3:5.

10. Proverbs 6:23.

11. Water: Genesis 1:6 (three times), 1:7 (twice). Firmament: 1:6, 1:7 (three times), 1:8.

resembles that of Divine inspiration ("light") becoming physical seed ("water") and finally a fetus ("firmament") in the mother's womb.

The numerical value of these three stages—*or* (207), *mayim* (90), *rakia* (380)—is 677, the value of *heichal hakodesh be'emtza*. The consciousness, *da'at*, of the Divine space we have created in our meditation, takes the "light" (the average value of the parameters of our space) and proceeds to draw it into our minds and hearts, converting it into "water" and "firmament," thus "conceiving" the light in our souls to be born as rectified emotions and behavioral characteristics that will lead us through life along the path of the Torah, the path of God.

22

Evening, Morning, and Noon[1]

The basis for praying three times a day is the verse in Psalms: "Evening, morning, and noon do I converse...."[2] "Converse" is a synonym for "pray."[3]

In its most literal sense, the phrase "evening, morning, and noon" need not necessarily refer to three distinct prayers, each limited in its extent of time, but may well be understood to imply a constant state of prayer, just as evening becomes morning and morning becomes noon, each overlapping and connecting to the other. So we see how the three daily prayers (as prescribed by the sages) strive to be constant.

Significantly, the numerical values of the words for "evening" (ערב, *erev*, 272), "morning" (בקר, *boker*, 302), and "noon" (צהרים, *tzohoraim*, 345) together equal that of the word for "meditation" (התבוננות, *hitbonenut*, 919). Meditation is surely an ideal, continuous state of mind. Even more remarkable is the fact that the numerical values of the "inner" letters, those "inside" (that is, not counting the first and last letters of) the three words for "evening" (the *reish* of *erev*, ערב, 200), "morning" (the *kuf* of *boker*, בקר, 100), and "noon" (the *hei reish yud* of *tzohoraim*, צהרים, 215) together equal that of the

---

1. See p. 74.

2. Psalms 55:18. See Rashi *ad loc.*; *Berachot* 20b.

3. *Ibid.* 26b.

word for "prayer" (*tefilah*, תפלה, 515). We thus see that prayer is the "inside," the inner experience, of meditation!

Analyzing the Biblical names for the three times of prayer (that strive to become one constant state of prayer) will shed additional light on the Divine space-time of our meditation. We shall see that space and time themselves are intrinsically related:

The first word, "evening" (*erev*) from which comes the name of the evening prayer (*aravit* or *ma'ariv*), shares the same root in Hebrew as "west" (*ma'arav*), for the west is the direction of sunset, as mentioned above. Thus, we may infer that the evening prayer (or the consciousness of evening in general) corresponds to the constant commandment of the *back*, to guard one's thoughts. The ensuing darkness of night alludes in Kabbalah to the *left*, and the north (*tzafon*), which in Hebrew means "concealed" or "hidden," as in the darkness of night. Evening-night is the time to protect oneself from physical/moral enemies and overcome foreign fears ("fears of night"[4]) by fearing only God. Thus, the evening prayer is associated, in particular, with the third "unit" described above, the unit of north and west.

The second word, "morning" (*boker*), the morning prayer (commonly referred to as *shacharit*, from *shachar*, which also means "morning," or "morning star"), is the prayer of sunrise, the prayer of the east, the *front*. According to the sages, this is the prayer instituted by Abraham, the man of love, all of whose journeys were to the south,[5] the *right* (the

---

4. Song of Songs 3:8.

5. Genesis 12:9.

direction that corresponds to the attribute of love in the soul). Abraham was the first to meditate on the unity of God in creation, to know the Creator of the universe, from which he gave birth in his soul to the emotion of love—"...GOD is our God; GOD is one. And you shall love GOD...."

Kabbalah and Hassidism speak of 42 journeys of the soul in this world, corresponding to the 42 journeys of the Jewish people from Egypt to the Promised Land. All of life's journeys, as the journeys of the first Jew, Abraham, are directed southward, to love. This is most beautifully alluded to by the fact that in the Five Books of Moses the root "to love" appears exactly 42 times!

Thus, the morning prayer corresponds, in particular, to the second "unit" described above, the unit of east and south.

The word used here for the afternoon prayer (*tzohoraim*; the common name of the afternoon prayer is *minchah*, which means "gift," not directly relating to its time in the day) implies "high noon." At this time of day, the sun is above one's head. This symbolizes the consciousness of the manifest presence of God, the Divine luminary, *above* us. This is the consciousness of *above*, the consciousness of the first of the Ten Commandments, the first of the six constant commandments of the Torah.

Together with the awareness of God on high is the awareness of man below. In the middle of our workday, we must pause to remember that we should not rely on any source of livelihood other than God. We must remember that all is a gift of God, and give all that we have received back to God, so to speak, by acknowledging and giving thanks for all He bestows upon us. (*Minchah*, the name of the afternoon prayer means "gift," as stated. Giving thanks is the service of the *sefirah* of *hod*, which means "thanksgiving," the direction of *below*, corresponding to the constant commandment that we should not believe in other gods.) This is the implication of the second of the Ten Commandments. Thus, the afternoon prayer corresponds, in particular, to the first "unit" of our meditation, the unit of *above* and *below*. Thus, through the daily cycle of our prayers, space and time merge to become one.

To summarize:

evening (*Ma'ariv*)	west (back)	guarding thoughts
	north (left)	fearing God
morning (*Shacharit*)	east (front)	unifying God
	south (right)	loving God
afternoon (*Minchah*)	above	believing in God
	below	serving God alone (denying idolatry)

We have seen that the first spatial unit of meditation is *above-below* and the last is north-south. According to the order of the day, beginning with night (as in the account of creation in which evening precedes morning), the last spatial unit of meditation, north-west, comes first, while the first unit, *above-below*, comes last. Thus, in the daily cycle, the dimension of time, the order intrinsic to space is reversed. This phenomenon itself reflects the perfect, complementary nature of the union of space and time. The innate logic of space meets and links to the innate logic of time. It now becomes clear that when we stated above that, in a certain sense, the last constant commandment of guarding one's thoughts comes first, we were referring to the way it appears in reference to the time frame of the Divine service of prayer—evening, morning, and noon.

Indeed, prayer is the seventh commandment, corresponding to *malchut*, which is symbolized in Kabbalah by a mirror that reflects light back to its source. In the process of reflecting light, *malchut*, the seventh level, ascends to link and unite with the sixth level, *yesod*, corresponding to the constant commandment of guarding one's thoughts.

23

The Limit Process[1]

We have identified five explicit stages in the zero-to-infinite progression of the commandment of prayer (which in mathematical terms would be called a "limit process," approaching a state of continuum):

- In the Written Torah, we are not commanded to pray.
- In the Written Torah, we are commanded to pray, but only in times of need.
- In the Written Torah, we are commanded to pray daily.
- In the Oral Torah, we are commanded to pray three times daily.
- "Would it be that man pray continuously."

These five stages of progression may be seen to correspond to five descending levels of consciousness. The first stage implies that the Divine service of prayer is so great that it cannot be prescribed for all. In true prayer to God, we reach a state of total self-sacrifice, thereby revealing the super-conscious root of our soul. This level corresponds to the *sefirah* of *keter*, the super-conscious, the tip of the *yud* of the unique Name of God, *Havayah*. In the creative process, this level is referred to in Kabbalah as *or*, "light."

---

1. See p. 74

To pray only in times of need, in times of trouble, implies the level of consciousness necessary to transform "trouble" (*tzarah*) into "brilliance" (*tzohar*), as taught by the Ba'al Shem Tov.[2] This level of consciousness is referred to in Kabbalah as *mochin d'Abba*, consciousness of "father"— *chochmah* ("wisdom"). The *sefirah* of *chochmah* corresponds to the *yud* of the Name *Havayah*. In the creative process, this level is referred to as *mayim*, "water." Water represents the spiritual ability to flow freely from permutation to permutation, to transform reality by rearranging the letters by which it is created. This opinion is expressed by Nachmanides, whose soul-root, according to the Arizal, originates in *chochmah*.

The injunction to pray daily implies spiritual regularity. This is the level of *mochin d'Ima*, consciousness of "mother"— *binah* ("understanding"). The *sefirah* of *binah* corresponds to the higher *hei* of the Name *Havayah*. In the creative process, this level is referred to as *rakia* ("firmament"), symbolizing the rigidity of regularity. This opinion is expressed by Maimonides, whose soul-root, according to the Arizal, originates in *binah*.

The three levels of *or*, *mayim*, and *rakia*, which were discussed at length previously, correspond to the three opinions regarding the commandment of prayer as required by the Written Torah. Indeed, in Kabbalah, it is explained that they correspond to the first three *sefirot* of *keter*, *chochmah*, and *binah*, which in turn correspond to the tip of the *yud*, the *yud*, and the higher *hei* of God's essential Name, *Havayah*.

---

2. See *Keter Shem Tov*, addendum 3.

The injunction of the Oral Torah to pray three times daily implies the need to rectify, through prayer—"the service of the heart"—the three essential emotions of the heart: love, fear, and mercy. These three emotions correspond to the three forefathers of the Jewish people—Abraham, Isaac, and Jacob—who first instituted the three daily prayers. This level corresponds to the *vav* of the Name *Havayah*, signifying the emotions of the heart. In the context of the heart, the forefathers reflect "father"-consciousness, and so reflect in the soul the creative level of water (which, as stated above, relates to *chochmah*, father, the beginning point of the right axis of the *sefirot*, whose nature is to descend, as is the nature of water). As an emotive attribute, water symbolizes love, the first and all-inclusive emotion of the heart. In praying three times daily, we flow freely from emotion to emotion, rectifying each at its given time.

Finally, "Would it be that man pray continuously" corresponds to the ideal state of prayer, the consummately rectified consciousness of *malchut* ("kingdom"), of which King David says in Psalms, "and I *am* prayer." This level of consciousness corresponds to the final *hei* of the Name *Havayah*, whose ultimate root is in the innermost realm of the super-conscious *keter*, the "unknowable head" of faith, as it is said: "the end is wedged in the beginning."[3] Here, not only is the pure light of the creative process reflected in the soul, but so is the Divine luminary, or source of light (*ma'or*), Himself.

To summarize:

---

3. *Sefer Yetzirah* 1:7.

tip of *yud*	*keter*	In the Written Torah, we are not commanded to pray.	*or* light
yud	*chochmah*	In the Written Torah, we are commanded to pray, but only in times of need.	*mayim* water
hei	*binah*	In the Written Torah, we are commanded to pray daily.	*rakia* firmament
vav	emotions	In the Oral Torah, we are commanded to pray three times daily.	*mayim* reflection of water
hei	*malchut*	"Would it be that man pray continuously."	*ma'or* reflection of source of light

24

The Miracle of Prayer[1]

It is told of many great *tzadikim* ("righteous people") that their devoted self-sacrifice in prayer was so great that only "miraculously" did they remain alive after prayer. One of the great disciples of the Ba'al Shem Tov, Rabbi Pinchas of Koretz, would part from his wife every morning before going to the synagogue to pray, not knowing if he would return.

And so we find in the words of the Ba'al Shem Tov himself:[2]

> It is thanks to God's great kindness that people remain alive after praying. In the natural course of events, death would have to result from exhausting all strength [in prayer] by exerting oneself so much in concentrating on all the great mystical intentions.
>
> Before praying, have in mind that you are prepared to die from [concentrating so intensely on] the [mystical] intentions while praying. Some concentrate so intensely that it would be natural for them to die after reciting [just] two or three words before God, blessed be He.
>
> Bearing this in mind, say to yourself: "Why would I have any ulterior motive or pride from my prayer

---

1. See p. 75.
2. *Tzava'at HaRibash* 35, 42 (ed. *Kehot*).

when I am prepared to die after two or three
words?"

Indeed, it is because of God's great kindness that He
gives [man] the strength to complete the prayer and
remain alive.

From this teaching of the Ba'al Shem Tov, we may
gain new insight into the essence of the commandment of
prayer as we have described it: prayer is a spiritual
progression from zero-to-infinity state. Inasmuch as we are
intended "to live by"[3] the commandments of the Torah and
"not die by them,"[4] it would seem that the Torah could not
command us to endanger our lives in intense prayer. (For this
very reason, animal sacrifice is commanded in the Torah in
place of sacrificing one's own self.) Indeed, all our intense
prayers are miracles in that we remain alive. Little by little, as
we become accustomed to experiencing such miracles, our
conscious state of prayer strives to become constant.

---

3. Leviticus 18:5.

4. *Yoma* 85b.

25

Ritual Baths, the Land of Israel, and the Sukah[1]

These six ascending levels of holiness, which correspond to the six constant commandments of the Torah, and thereby to the six directions of space (themselves corresponding to the six emotive *sefirot* from *chesed* to *yesod*), correspond, as well, to the "six levels of ritual baths [*mikva'ot*]."[2]

The Ba'al Shem Tov, in outlining the "intentions" (*kavanot*, "focused thoughts") a person is to have upon immersing in the purifying waters of the *mikveh*,[3] explains that the "six levels of ritual baths" correspond to the six directions (the six *sefirot* from *chesed* to *yesod*) that surround the person who immerses. To be purified, he or she must be totally encompassed by the waters of the *mikveh*; not even one hair may remain outside.

"The Land of Israel is pure and its ritual baths are pure."[4] (On the spiritual plane, purity is the state of consciousness conducive to the revelation of the Divine.) The

---

1. See p. 83.

2. *Mikva'ot* 1:1.

3. See *Keter Shem Tov*, beginning.

4. *Mikva'ot* 8:1

Land of Israel is like its ritual baths: both are pure. Just as we are to fully enter and become encompassed by the atmosphere of the Land of Israel, so are we, when immersing in a *mikveh*, to become fully encompassed by its purifying waters.

Here is an additional instance, a physical example, of "Living in Divine Space." The purifying waters of the *mikveh* encompass us from all sides. In particular, however, the secret of the *mikveh* is related to the west; the most common name for "west" in the Torah is "sea" (*yam*), for the Mediterranean Sea is the western border of the Land of Israel. The sun sets into the sea, immersing, as it were, in its waters. The purification of the *mikveh*, thus, firstly purifies our mind from foreign, negative thoughts. We return to a womb-like state, where all is good.

In addition, it is explained that the most fundamental intention of immersion is that *tevilah* ("immersion") permutes to spell *ha-bitul* ("selflessness"). To become pure, to be born anew from the "amniotic fluid" of the spiritual womb, we must nullify our ego. This relates to the constant commandment of fear, the Divine consciousness of *left* (north), which brings us to selflessness, as has been explained. Thus, in particular, the immersion in the Divine space of the *mikveh* alludes to the "unit" of left-back (north-west).

And so, in particular, entering the Land of Israel (with all of its ascending levels of holiness, corresponding to all the six constant commandments of the Torah), walking on its holy ground, and becoming encompassed by its enlightening atmosphere, alludes to the unit of front-right (east-south).

Rabbi Nachman of Breslov used to say, "Wherever I go, I am headed toward the Land of Israel." The Land of

Israel is in the *front* of our consciousness always. As well, the
Land of Israel is referred to in the Torah as "the right,"[5] the
direction of love.

(More than with regard to any other direction of
space, *right* connects space to time. "Right" (*yamin*) is used as
well to mean "days" [*yamin*[6]]. Of Abraham, the soul
symbolizing the right, it is said, "having come of days."[7]
Love, more than any other emotion of the heart, unites space
and time. For this reason, it is said, "the world is built with
chesed [the emotion of love, the *right*]."[8] "The world" [*olam*]
means, in the Torah, both the entire universe of space and
the eternity of time.)

There is one additional physical commandment in the
Torah that requires "entering"—the *mitzvah* of *sukah* (the
commandment to dwell in a booth during the Festival of
Sukot). The covering of the *sukah* is explicitly referred to in
the *Zohar*[9] as "the shadow of faith." We enter a *sukah* to be
protected, by its shade, from the noonday sun.[10] Thus, the
sukah alludes, in particular, as does the afternoon prayer, to
the spatial unit of *above-below*, corresponding to the first two
of the Ten Commandments.

---

5. Rashi on Genesis 31:18.

6. See Daniel 12:13.

7. Genesis 24:1.

8. Psalms 89:3.

9. 3:103a.

10. See Isaiah 4:6.

To summarize:

mikveh	*back*/west
	left/north
the Land of Israel	*front*/east
	right/south
sukah	*above*
	below

26

Marital Union[1]

If we analyze the six constant commandments as three pairs, we see here that the first pair of *below-above* corresponds to the Land of Israel itself (*below*, the prohibition against idolatry), the lowest level of holiness, and the Holy of Holies (*above*, belief in God), the apex of holiness. This is in accord with the statement in *Sefer Yetzirah*[2] that "The end is wedged in the beginning and the beginning in the end." The two levels of holiness that correspond to the "cities" of Israel— the walled cities and Jerusalem—form the pair of west-north (shielding the mind from negative thoughts, and fear of God). And lastly, the two levels of holiness that correspond to the Temple Mount and the Temple form the pair of south-east (love of God and unity of God).

The Prophet Isaiah[3] metaphorically describes the relationship of the Jewish people to the Land of Israel as the marital union of the people (the groom) to the land (the bride). In every Hassidic marriage ceremony, we may identify six levels of ascent, which correspond to the six levels of holiness described above:

---

1. See p. 85.

2. 1:7.

3. 62:4-5.

1. The engagement of the groom and bride (*tena'im* or *vort*) is like entering the Land of Israel in general. One stops thinking of others (that is, stops considering other possible marriage partners), concentrating solely on one's predestined betrothed (*bashert*).

2. Before the wedding ceremony, the guests greet the bride and groom (*kabalat panim*). Great care is taken that the couple be shielded from seeing each other at the wedding hall prior to the beginning of the wedding ceremony (this is the culmination of the week prior to the marriage, in which the couple refrain from seeing one another). Their separate "domains" at this point are similar to the separate, walled cities of Israel. Their concentrated intention is not on each other but rather on God, the third partner of marriage, as they "invite" Him (together with the righteous people of past generations) to attend the wedding ceremony and bless them.

3. Next, the groom goes to cover the bride's face with a veil (*badeken*), at once uplifting her toward him[4] while simultaneously, by his having hidden her face from him, producing in both an aura of awe (a bashful fear, the highest level of fear). This is like entering the city of Jerusalem (the city of consummate fear, *Yeru-shalem*).

4. Then, under the canopy, the bride circles the groom seven times (*hakafot*). This resembles the custom of circling the Temple Mount, walking around the Temple site. Here, the bride arouses her great, infinite love for her groom, which in turn, "as water reflects face to face, so does one's heart

---

4. *Ma'amar Lechah Dodi* 5687.

find reflection in another's,"[5] arouses the great love of the groom for his bride.

5. The actual betrothal of the bride by the groom (*kidushin*) is like entering the Temple itself. Spiritually, the couple has become one.

6. Then, the couple proceeds to the seclusion room (*cheder yichud*). This is like entering the Holy of Holies. Here, God, the third partner of marriage, and the couple consummately unite; here is revealed the absolute "I am that I am."

To summarize:

back	*tena'im*	engagement	Land of Israel
below	*kabalat panim*	reception	walled cities
left	*bedeken*	covering the bride's face	Jerusalem
right	*hakafot*	bride circling groom	Temple Mount
front	*kidushin*	betrothal	Temple
above	*cheder yichud*	seculsion	Holy of Holies

---

5. Proverbs 27:19.

27

Three Pairs[1]

Let us examine the structure of the six verses that express the six continuous commandments, noting the number of words and letters that form each:

Verse		words	letters
I am GOD, your God, who has taken you out of the land of Egypt, out of the house of bondage.	אנכי ה' אלהיך אשר הוצאתיך מארץ מצרים מבית עבדים.	9	41
You shall have no other gods before Me.	לא יהיה לך אלהים אחרים על פני.	7	23
Hear O Israel, GOD is our God, GOD is one.	שמע ישראל ה' אלהינו ה' אחד.	6	25
And you shall love GOD your God with all your heart, and with all your soul, and with all your might.	ואהבת את ה' אלהיך בכל לבבך ובכל נפשך ובכל מאדך.	10	39
And now, O Israel, what does GOD, your God, ask of you, but to fear...	ועתה ישראל מה ה' אלהיך שאל מעמך כי אם ליראה...	10	36
And you shall not stray after your heart and after your eyes...	ולא תתורו אחרי לבבכם ואחרי עיניכם...	6	28

We see here a most amazing phenomenon:

---

1. See pp. 29, 43, 51, and 67.

The first two verses—the first two verses of the Ten Commandments—join together to form a unit of 16 words and 64 letters.

The third and fourth verses also join together to form a unit of 16 words and 64 letters, exactly as did the first unit!

And the fifth and six verses (the fifth until the word "to fear" and the sixth until the word "your eyes") combine to form a unit that once more contains 16 words and 64 letters!

$16 = 4^2 (= 2^4)$; $64 = 4$ times $16 = 8^2 (= 4^3 = 2^6)$. In Kabbalah, a square number (or a number to any power above 2) manifests a perfect state of inter-inclusion (the holistic principle that each of the elements reflects all of the elements). A single text, or two or more related texts, that contains such a number of words or letters manifests perfection. Such a text or texts can then be given a simple, symmetric geometric form—a square (or cube, etc.). In our case, the "completion" is consummate, for both the number of words and the number of letters are squares (as well as higher powers of 2) and the ratio between the words and the letters is 1:4 $(4 = 2^2)$.

This is the ideal ratio of words to letters in the Torah, as seen with respect to the most important word of the Torah, the essential Name of God, *Havayah*, called by the sages the "four-letter Name," emphasizing the fact that this 1 word possesses 4 letters.

In Kabbalah, we are taught that any textual unit in the Torah possesses (in addition to its number of letters, words, numerical value, etc.) an additional unit value, the *kolel* (literally, "all-inclusive" value), a manifestation of the unitary, all-encompassing light that connects together the individual elements of the textual unit. In this case, the linking together of the two verses in each set manifests an additional $1 = 1^2$.

We thus have three squares associated with each textual unit: 1^2, the *kolel*; 4^2, the number of words; and 8^2, the number of letters. The three square roots, in the order 1-8-4, when translated into letters, spell the word for "one" (*echad*). The sum of the three squares is itself a square: $1^2 \perp 8^2 \perp 4^2 = 81 = 9^2$. $81 = Anochi$, meaning "I," the first, all-inclusive word of the Ten Commandments, representing God's very essence, as explained above.

The average value of letters of the first two commandments is 32, the numerical value of the word for "heart" in Hebrew (*lev*), alluding to the fact that these commandments are the "duties of the heart." 32 equals 1 times 8 times 4.

The average value of the number of letters of all 6 verses, the six "duties of the heart," is also 32, the numerical value of the word "heart" (*lev*)! 6 times $32 = 192$, the numerical value of the word for "rhythm" (*ketzev*). From this we may infer that constant awareness of the 192 letters that compose the six verses of the six constant commandments of the Torah—"Living in Divine Space"—creates life's rhythm.

We noted earlier that the Ten Commandments appear twice in the Torah. Thus, the first unit formed by the first two of the Ten Commandments, possessing 16 words and 64 letters, can be counted twice. We thus arrive at 4 units of 16 words and 64 letters, a total of 64 words and 256 letters. $64 = 8^2$, $256 = 16^2$ ($= 4^4 = 2^8$).

By counting the letters of the Torah we have thus constructed a four-dimensional space-time hypercube of 4^4.

The number 256 (4⁴) is the total number of wings of
the 4 "living beings" (angels) of the Divine chariot in the
vision of Ezekiel. Each living being possesses 4 faces; each
face itself reflects all 4 faces—16 faces for each living being;
each face possesses 4 wings, a total of 64 wings for each
being, 256 wings for all 4.[2]

We here observe the supreme importance of 4, the
first manifest square number (although 1 is 1 squared, it is
not manifest as a square). The number 256 is here (in the
phenomenon of the number of wings of Ezekiel's living
beings) explicitly represented as 4⁴. It is noteworthy that the
numerical value of the very word for "numerology" in the
Torah, *gematria*, is 273, the same as that for "four" (*arba*)!
(This explains, as well, the relationship of numerology—
gematria—to *geometry*. The number 4, as represented by four
dots, possesses the ideal geometric form, a square. Thus, the
word *gematria* alludes to the study of numbers as portrayed by
geometric forms in general and squares in particular.)

In Kabbalah, we are taught that all of reality exists on
four general levels, the four worlds of *Atzilut* ("Emanation"),
Beriah ("Creation"), *Yetzirah* ("Formation"), and *Asiyah*
("Action"). In our meditation, our space-time hypercube may
thus be multiplied by 4 (in prayer, we ascend from world to
world, from one space-time model to a higher, parallel one).
We thereby reach a total of 256 words and 1024 (= 32² = 4⁵
= 2¹⁰) letters.

This number—1024—is the exact number of letters of
the full reading of the *Shema*: the three Torah-sections contain

2. *Targum Yonatan* on Ezekiel 1:6.

exactly 1000 (= 10^3) letters, and the sentence added by the sages to follow the first verse of "Hear, O Israel..."— "Blessed be the Name of His glorious kingdom forever and ever"—is composed of an additional 24 letters! (This was also the measurement of the altar in the Holy Temple, 32 by 32 cubits.) By combining the consciousness of all four worlds, we have now entered a ten-dimensional hypercube (2^{10}).

APPENDIX

Seven Guided Meditations

*(as recorded on
the Gal Einai Meditation Website:
www.inner-meditation.org)*

1

Love: The Power of Creation

Love is the Divine power of creation. Let us focus on arousing the power of love in our souls. Let the word for "love" in Hebrew, *ahavah,* reverberate in our hearts and on our lips. *A-ha-vah.*

Now, let us picture the word *ahavah*:

אהבה

The four letters of *ahavah*—*alef, hei, beit,* and *hei*—are the first, fifth, second, and fifth letters of the Hebrew alphabet. Together, they equal the number 13. Thirteen is also the numerical value of the word for "one" in Hebrew, *echad*:

אחד

Love is feeling the essence of oneness with our beloved; a feeling that impels us to become close and to unite with our beloved. Let us feel one with God the Creator and with all of His creation.

Now, let us continue to meditate upon the word *ahavah*. Its four letters are an acronym for the phrase, "The light of the Holy One, Blessed be He": *Or Hakadosh Baruch Hu.*

אוֹר הַקָּדוֹשׁ בָּרוּךְ הוּא

With God's infinite light, His love for all, He continuously creates the world anew. So may we walk in His ways and emanate from our souls the creative power of love.

2

Breathing Joy

King David concludes the book of Psalms with the verse, "Every soul shall praise God, Hallelujah." In Hebrew, the word for "soul" (*neshamah*) also means "breath" (*neshimah*). And so the verse reads, "Every *breath* shall praise God, Hallelujah."

Let us breathe deeply, and praise God with every breath. With every breath, I feel Your Presence. With every breath I express my infinite gratitude to You and Your gift of life.

Now, let us breathe joy into our lives. The word in Hebrew for "joy" is *chedvah*. It is composed of four letters, *chet*, *dalet*, *vav*, and *hei*, whose numerical values are 8, 4, 6, and 5, respectively:

חדוה

Each breath is composed of four stages: inhaling, holding, exhaling, and resting.

First, inhale 8. Count in your heart from one to eight while inhaling.

Now, hold for a count of 4.

Then, exhale for a count of 6.

Finally, rest for a count of 5.

What is important is that you breathe deeply in a meditative state. The ratio of 8:4:6:5 must be maintained, but the exact length of each unit of count is not crucial. For each individual, it should flow naturally.

ח	*chet*	count 8	inhaling
ד	*dalet*	count 4	holding
ו	*vav*	count 6	exhaling
ה	*hei*	count 5	resting

To experience life is to experience joy. This is the joy of feeling my Creator blowing into my nostrils the breath of life. For this I praise Him with every breath.

3

Living in Divine Space

Let us construct around us, in meditation, a Divine space, a spiritual sanctuary. Space possesses six directions. Each direction corresponds to a continuous state of consciousness as prescribed by one of the six constant commandments of the Torah.

First, become aware of the Divine space *above* you. This is the consciousness of the first of the Ten Commandments: "I am GOD, your God, who has taken you out of the land of Egypt, out of the house of bondage." This is the consciousness of God's Omnipotence, His Omnipresence and His Divine Providence.

Now, become aware of the Divine space *below* you. This is the consciousness of the second of the Ten Commandments; not to believe in any other god beside Him. This is the consciousness of the One God of Israel. He, and only He is our sole Provider and Sustainer. There is no other one beside Him; no one on whom to rely except Him.

Now, become aware of the Divine space in *front* of you. This is the consciousness of God's absolute Unity. He is the One, the only One, and unique in the paradoxical essence of His Oneness. For His Oneness is in truth an imponderable state of Oneness. This is what we experience in our declaration of faith, "Hear O Israel, GOD is our God, GOD is One."

Now, become aware of the Divine space to your *right*. This is the consciousness and the experience of love for God; a love that encompasses love for all, with all of one's heart, all of one's soul and all of one's might.

Now, become aware of the Divine space to your *left*. This is the consciousness of the awe experienced in the presence of the Infinite One, blessed be He. May this awe serve to nullify all of our negative energies, which derive ultimately from our over-inflated ego.

Now, become aware of the Divine space to your *back*. This is the awareness of our liability to be attacked by foreign, negative thoughts and energies. We must continuously post a guard at our back door to prevent those enemies from entering. This is the consciousness of staying on guard, always ready to fight against evil. We are commanded in the Torah to guard God's sanctuary from all foreign invaders. In merit of this final, continuous state of consciousness, we will experience the fulfillment of the verse, "And I shall make the spirit of impurity pass away from the earth."

Into our own Divine space that we have now constructed around ourselves, our own personal messianic spark will reveal itself. May we become inspired to redeem ourselves, with God's help, from our own state of exile, and to redeem all of the world around us.

4

Motion: The Flame of the Candle

Let us meditate on the words of King Solomon in the
Book of Proverbs:

The soul of man is the candle of GOD.

The flame of a candle is continuously in motion,
continuously alive, swaying back and forth. Sometimes, the
sway is intense. At other times, it is so gentle that it is hardly
noticeable to the eye. So does the living soul of man, the
candle of God, sway back and forth, always aspiring to return
to its Divine source, the Infinite Light of God.

In this world, the soul is clothed in the body. Thus,
the sway of the soul produces an equivalent sway in the body.

Let us now stand erect, and sway back and forth. First,
let us sway from front to back. This direction of swaying
reflects the male dimension of our soul. Then, let us sway
from right to left. This direction of swaying reflects the
female dimension of our soul. When standing and swaying
from right to left, let your body turn around the pivot point
of your waist. (When sitting, the right to left sway is without
this turning effect.)

The soul's natural phenomenon of swaying, like a
living candle, reaches its peak when we learn God's Torah
and pray to Him from the depth of our hearts.

May our spark of God, the flame of our souls that always aspires to return and unite with God's Infinite Light, be awakened and aroused. May it never be extinguished. In every direction, we sway towards You.

5

Modeh Ani: Expressing Thanks

Each morning we wake up and thank God for returning our soul to us. The first words that we say upon waking are:

I thank You, ever-living King,
for compassionately returning my soul to me.
How great is Your faithfulness.

In Hebrew:

*Modeh ani l'fanecha, melech chai v'kayam,
shehechezarta bi nishmati b'chemlah,
rabah emunatecha.*

To offer thanks, to express our most sincere gratitude, is to feel like an empty vessel. Would it not be for the loving-kindness and compassion of the Giver, we would remain empty, possessing nothing. In our case, this means we would not be alive. In true humility, we experience the presence of the Eternal King standing *above* us. Every night before sleep, we give our tired and worn-out souls back to God. Every morning, we receive our souls anew, refreshed and full of energy. How great is God's faithfulness!

Our sages teach us that sleep is one sixtieth of death. God receives a nearly expired soul, and He gives it back to us, reborn. Just as in this world, He is faithful to us and we rely

216

on Him every day of our lives, and indeed every moment, to constantly renew our souls, the life of our bodies, so will He be faithful to us and do we rely on Him to resurrect the dead in the World to Come.

With the thought and intention of "I thank You," we begin our day. This thought accompanies us, always engraved in our consciousness, the whole day long.

6

The Four-Letter Name

God's essential, ineffable Name is generally referred to as the Tetragrammaton, so called after the connotation given it by the sages, the "four-letter Name." In Hebrew, it is called "the Name *Havayah*."

Although the essence of this Name transcends all meaning, it comes from the Hebrew root which means "to be," or "to bring into being." The Name *Havayah* is the eternal being, the Divine power that continuously brings all of reality into being.

Though we are forbidden to pronounce the Name *Havayah* as it is written, we may meditate on its four letters, *yud*, *hei*, *vav*, and *hei*. (Indeed, all Kabbalistic focused "intentions" center around this meditation):

$$ \text{ה-ו-ה-י} $$

These four letters correspond to the four worlds of creation: Emanation, Creation, Formation and Action, which in turn correspond to four general levels of consciousness.

First, meditate on the first letter of the Name *Havayah*, the letter *yud*:

י

This is the consciousness of God's absolute Omnipresence. There is no other beside Him, and there is no place without Him. "Hear O Israel, GOD [*Havayah*] is our God, GOD [*Havayah*] is One."

Now, meditate on the second letter of the Name *Havayah,* the first *hei:*

ה

This is the consciousness of the Divine creative process. Experience the whole universe, yourself included, being created this moment *ex nihilo,* here and now.

Next, meditate on the third letter of the Name *Havayah,* the *vav:*

ו

This is the consciousness of being a part of a larger whole. Experience the entire cosmos as one grand being. No part exists in and of itself. To take hold of a part is to take hold of the whole.

Now, meditate on the fourth letter of the Name *Havayah,* the second *hei:*

ה

This is the consciousness of the individual feeling himself or herself alone, independent and separate from all others. Assume full responsibility, for yours is the power of free choice.

Finally, come to the realization that all four levels of consciousness are essentially one. Say once more:

Hear O Israel, GOD is our God, GOD is One.

Shema Yisrael, Adonai Eloheinu, Adonai echad.

7

Shabbat: Peace, Blessing, and Pleasure

The relationship of the Jewish soul to the holy day of Shabbat is one of betrothal. Shabbat is the soul-mate of the Jewish people. The Jewish soul is married to Shabbat.

By observing Shabbat, on the spiritual plane as well as on the physical plane, we come to experience the Divine mystery of Shabbat throughout the entire week, ever anticipating the arrival of the consummate Shabbat experience on the day of Shabbat itself.

Let us now meditate on the word Shabbat:

שבת

In the *Zohar*, we learn that the word *Shabbat* is in fact a Name of God.

The three letters of Shabbat, the *shin*, the *beit*, and the *tav*, stand for three words:

"peace"	*Sh*alom	שלום
"blessing"	*B*rachah	ברכה
"pleasure"	*T*a'anug	תענוג

Our sages teach us that peace is the vessel that we must create in order to receive the light of Divine blessing, the blessing of all good things: children, good health, and prosperity. The essential experience of Shabbat, the experience of God's light of blessing entering our vessel of peace, is the experience of Divine pleasure.

On Shabbat, we greet one another with the words:

Shabbat shalom
A peaceful Shabbat

or:

Shabbat shalom umevorach
A peaceful and blessed Shabbat.

May we all achieve the consummate Shabbat experience of peace, blessing, and Divine pleasure.

Endnotes

Preface

1. Address of 12 Tamuz, 5739. In part, this was in response to the growing interest in Eastern systems of meditation, which were then being popularized in the Western world.

2. The Rebbe pointed out that such techniques would likely prove detrimental for a disciplined Torah scholar or anyone else whose mind has been conditioned to fast, multi-dimensional thinking.

3. Psalms 16:8.

4. Proverbs 5:16; Letter of the Ba'al Shem Tov to his brother-in-law, Rabbi Gershon of Kitov, published at the end of *Ben Porat Yosef* and excerpted at the beginning of *Keter Shem Tov*.

5. Following his address, the Rebbe turned to a number of clinical psychologists in America and Israel to develop a form of "kosher" Jewish meditation. The Rebbe requested specifically that they focus on the first level of meditation listed above—general relaxation techniques. The Rebbe's immediate concern was to provide people, who might otherwise stray into meditative techniques based on Eastern religions, with a "kosher" alternative free of idolatrous practices, and he reasoned that too much Jewish mystical content might confuse them.

The Rebbe also noted that when possible, it is best to first separate the Jew who has fallen into non-kosher indoctrination from it before teaching him the Torah in general and the mysteries of the Torah in particular. When this is not possible, however, the Torah instructs us that in order to save a Jewish soul, we *must* risk the possibility of "throwing a stone to Mercury" (i.e., giving an influx of life-force to idolatry) by teaching the Jew the Torah and its mysteries (see *Shulchan Aruch HaRav, Talmud Torah* 4:3; *Kuntres Acharon ad loc.*).

It is now clear that the reason most of the attempts of those professionals to whom the Rebbe turned were not successful was that the systems they developed were not sufficiently attractive to the spiritual senses of those seeking respite in meditation.

True, many people turn to meditation simply in order to relax, but even so, the attraction of any specific meditation technique lies in its being based on some religious or quasi-religious system that claims greater depth than that claimed by modern psychology. Therefore, a meditation system professing to be *Jewish* but not based on Kabbalah cannot address the masses, for consciously or unconsciously they sense that it lacks the depth they are seeking.

6. Recordings of some of Rabbi Ginsburgh's lectures on this system of meditation are available at the Gal Einai Website (www.inner-store.org).

In addition, the Gal Einai website features an associated site (www.inner-meditation.org) with recordings of Rabbi Ginsburgh guiding seven meditation sessions for beginners. (Although each meditation is appropriate at all times, the seven, as ordered here, may be seen to relate in particular to the seven days of the week.) The text of these meditations appears in the appendix. There, the meditation "Living in Divine Space," the topic of this book, is summarized and presented for the beginner in meditation 3. (This meditation corresponds, in particular, to the third day of creation, the day on which the earth was revealed and named, for it is the ground-level meditation. In Kabbalah, the third day of creation, corresponding to the Divine attribute of *tiferet*, "beauty," reflects the consciousness of all six spatial directions while emphasizing *frontal* consciousness. Here, this means achieving continual consciousness of the six constant commandments of the Torah, with special emphasis placed on the commandment to believe and know that God is absolutely One).

7. *Chagigah* 12b.

8. Indeed, all of the levels of meditation associated with the seven heavens are reflected in the most basic ground-level meditation of "Living in Divine Space," creating here, on earth, a spiritual sanctuary wherein we meet with God.

In particular, the firmament of *Zevul*, which contains the spiritual holy Temple ready to descend in fire from heaven, is clearly reflected in the spiritual sanctuary we construct around ourselves by retaining continuous consciousness of the six constant commandments of the Torah here on earth.

Furthermore, as the seven firmaments correspond in Kabbalah to the supernal *sefirot*, as do the Torah's six constant commandments together with the commandment of prayer (as will be described in detail in the text), clearly there must be parallels and correspondences between the firmaments and their content and the elements/*mitzvot* of "Living in Divine Space" (as we hope to expand upon in the future, please God).

In short, the meditation of "Living in Divine Space" encapsulates the essence of all the levels of Jewish meditation, as can be sensed by each individual according to his or her natural spiritual tendencies.

9. *The Hebrew Letters: Channels of Creative Consciousness* describes the meditative dimension of the Hebrew alphabet. This is the third level of Jewish meditation, corresponding to the second heaven (*Rakia*), as we have mentioned. *Sod Hashem Lireiav*, at present available only in Hebrew, describes meditation on God's essential, four-letter Name. This is the seventh level of meditation, corresponding to the sixth heaven (*Machon*).

In particular, *The Mystery of Marriage: How to Find True Love and Happiness in Married Life*, contains much material describing the practice and content of Jewish meditation, since true meditation is in fact a spiritual marriage between God and the meditator.

Incidentally, this is why, in classical Kabbalah, only married individuals were allowed to practice meditation. In order to understand and practice meditation, it is necessary to understand and be practiced in its consummate allegory, marriage, as reflected in the pervasive use of marital imagery in the classic texts of Kabbalah. Hassidism has succeeded in abstracting this explicit imagery, and therefore, since its advent, this restriction has been relaxed. But even so, it is certain that marriage enhances our ability to meditate effectively. (In fact, there remained Hassidic masters who frowned on unmarried people engaging in Hassidic meditation.)

10. In this vein, Rabbi Ginsburgh has also composed many meditative melodies. Some of these have been recorded and are available at the Gal Einai website.

11. Psalms 35:10.

12. As did King David (2 Samuel 6:14).

13. As is told of one of the great Hassidic masters, Rabbi Yaakov Yitzchak of Pshis'chah, known as "the Holy Jew."

14. In this vein, Rabbi Ginsburgh has developed a practice of meditative breathing exercises, postures, and movements to accompany meditation. This system has also been taught and practiced by many of his students for some time. This system is a further implementation of the Rebbe's call to create a "kosher" alternative to meditative and healing practices rooted in Eastern religions. The description of this system is so far available only in Hebrew.

A basic example of a Torah-based breathing exercise is presented in the Appendix, "Breathing Joy." A basic example of meditative movement, one most explicitly rooted in the Torah and Jewish tradition, is presented in the Appendix, "Motion: The Flame of the Candle."

15. See also #16, pp. 8-9; #17, p. 3; #18, pp. 6-7.

Introduction

1. Psalms 119:10. See Supplementary Essay #1, "To Seek God" (p. 95).

2. An analogy of Rabbi Dovber, the Maggid of Mezritch (?-1772), the successor to the Ba'al Shem Tov as the leader of the Hassidic Movement.

3. The sages teach that God Himself abides by the principles of the Torah (*Shemot Rabbah* 30:9). By giving the Torah to us, He shares with us His ways, teaching us how to make our ways His.

4. See Genesis 18:19; Judges 2:22; 2 Samuel 22:22; 2 Kings 21:22; Jeremiah 5:4-5; Hosea 14:10; Psalms 18:22, 25:4, 138:5; 2 Chronicles 17:6; see also *Ner Mitzvah veTorah Or*, introduction (2b).

5. See Supplementary Essay #2, "The Ways of God," p. 102.

6. Rabbi Dovber of Lubavtich, *Torat Chaim, Bereishit*, vol. 1, p. 65d; see *Malchut Yisrael*, vol. 1, pp. 159 ff.

7. *Ta'anit* 2a, based on Deuteronomy 11:13. See Supplementary Essay #3, "Pouring out the Heart" (p. 106).

8. The triplet of "point, line, area" possesses a parallel in Kabbalah: "point, spectrum, persona" (*Mavo She'arim*, 2:2:1; *Eitz Chaim* 31:6; *Imrei Binah* 74b ff). A spectrum or supernal light (*sefirah*) is a well-defined structure—a line; a persona (*partzuf*) is a fully developed expression of Divine life—an area.

9. In Hassidic thought (*HaYom Yom*, 20 *Tamuz*), it is explained that meditation possesses three stages, which themselves correspond to the progression of "point, line, area":

- study as preparation for meditation,
- meditation before prayer, and
- meditation during prayer.

Relative to one another, these are:

- a yet inanimate "point,"
- a dynamically animate "line," and
- a full experience—"area"—of Divine life.

As study in general is the "point" preceding the actual service of meditation, while studying we should try to retain an awareness of the initial point of meditation itself, which of course is the search for God (as in "with all my heart, I seek You"). In direct proportion to the sincerity and intensity of this focus will we succeed in progressing toward our goal.

If, at any time, the study becomes overwhelming, we always have the "point" to return to, as this "point" is its spark of life, never to be extinguished. It is what inspires us to reach deeper, more profound levels of understanding in all the stages of this process (see *Keter Shem Tov* 84 [11c], on Leviticus 6:6, "a continual fire shall burn on the altar; it shall not be extinguished").

Chapter One

1. Cf. *Sha'ar HaYichud VehaEmunah*, chapter 11: "they [the twenty-two Hebrew letters] are twenty-two different types of flow of life-force and powers, through which all upper and lower worlds were created...their form in writing reflects the depiction of the flow...." See at length *The Hebrew Letters: Channels of Creative Consciousness*.

2. *Kidushin* 30a: "Therefore the early sages were called *sofrim*, because they would *count* [*sofrim*] all the letters of the Torah...." In the endnotes of the coming chapters we, too, will count the letters of the verses appearing in our meditation, in order to understand from the numbers of their words and letters and their numerical values deeper meanings and allusions with regard to their inner content and teaching for us.

3. See *Likutei Moharan* 1:65.

4. Cf. the phrase אנא נפשי כתבית יהבית (*Shabbat* 105a, according to *Ein Yaakov*; cf. *Likutei Torah* 3:48d). See Supplementary Essay #4, "The Name of God," p. 108.

5. Deuteronomy 4:39. See Supplementary Essay #5, "Sinai Past and Present," p. 112.

6. *Kuntres Acharon* 4 (156b).

7. Rabbeinu Yonah, quoted in *Sefer HaChareidim*.

8. See Deuteronomy 8:18: "You shall remember GOD your God, that it is He who gives you power to succeed." This verse is referred to as the "remembrance of the Land of Israel," for it appears in the context of the Jewish people entering the Land of Israel, settling the land and eating its fruits. For Jewish consciousness, the Land of Israel is truly a Divine Space. And so, this verse and its message pertain especially to the meditation of "Living in Divine Space."

Chapter Two

1. Cf. *Mishnah Berurah, Biur Halachah* on the opening statement of Rabbi Moshe Isserles' *Mapah* on *Orach Chaim* 1:1, the beginning of the *Shulchan Aruch*, the Code of Jewish Law.

2. See Supplementary Essay #6, "The Commandments of God," p. 117.

3. See Supplementary Essay #7, "The Commandments: Spiritual and Physical," p. 120.

4. See Supplementary Essay #8, "The All-Inclusive Commandments," p. 123.

5. A popular medieval work that enumerates the 613 commandments of the Torah (based upon Maimonides' system of counting) and explains them both from a legal and a moral perspective.

6. Numbers 35:6.

7. See Supplementary Essay #9, "The Six Cities of Refuge," p. 126.

8. See Supplementary Essay #10, "The Cube and Pascal's Triangle," p. 129.

9. Deuteronomy 6:4.

10. *Tur, Orach Chaim* 61; *Beit Yosef ad loc.*

11. On the verse from the Book of Numbers (9:6)—"There were people who were impure through [contact with the corpse of] a human soul [literally, 'the soul of man' or 'the soul of *Adam*']"— the sages state (*Sukah* 25a) that they were those Jews who were carrying the coffin of Joseph in the desert.

In Kabbalah, we are taught that the numerical value of *Adam*, when calculated in the "progressive" system of numbering (*mispar kidmi*, the value of each letter taken as the sum of all the letters of the alphabet from *alef* to and including itself) equals the conventional numerical value of *Joseph* (156).

12. Psalms 109:4.

13. See Supplementary Essays #11, "The Archetypal Souls of Israel," p. 135., and #12, "The Hypercube," p. 140.

14. As though to say that it is the power of the right leg that takes one "uphill," while it is the power of the left leg that takes one "downhill."

15. The torso, the chest, represents the drive to move forward. The procreative organ represents the drive to find and unite with one's soul mate, who, according to Kabbalah, is initially connected to one's back side (as was Eve to Adam upon their creation; Adam and Eve were created connected "back to back" [*Berachot* 61a]), a symbol for one's unconscious.

16. The mouth's service of prayer corresponds to the relative *back* of the mouth, whereas the mouth's service of studying the Oral Torah (*Tikunei Zohar*, introduction, *s.v. Patach Eliahu*: "*malchut* is the mouth, it is called the Oral Torah") corresponds to the relative *front* of the mouth.

17. See Supplementary Essay #13, "The Six Remembrances," p. 144.

Chapter Three

1. Exodus 20:2. See Supplementary Essay #27, "Three Pairs," p. 201.

2. The fact that the possessive suffix ("your" in the singular) is attached to the Name of God indicates that God, the Redeemer, relates personally to each and every individual. Also, in the continuation of the verse, "who has taken *you* out of…," *you* is in the singular, to make the same point.

The sages teach us that the singular person in this verse indicates that God here addresses Moses in particular (*Yalkut Shimoni, Shemot* 392). Moses corresponds to the *sefirah* of *netzach*, the top of our meditative cube, corresponding to this constant commandment. In Kabbalah, addressing Moses means addressing the spark of Moses present in every Jewish soul, the ability of every soul to become conscious of the Divine through meditation (beginning with the meditation on the first of the Ten Commandments, the first of the six constant commandments of the Torah, as explained in *Tanya* (chapter 42).

3. Exodus 3:14. In the *Zohar* 3:11a, this verse is quoted and explained as follows: "'I am whom I am,' and am not alluded to by any Name or letter or tip of letter," meaning that God's very essence cannot be conveyed by any Name (a composite of holy letters), not even the unique Name *Havayah*. Only the simple faith of the Jewish soul—"an actual part of God above" (*Tanya*, ch. 2)—can relate to, "contain in itself," as it were, God's very essence. Divine Names, holy letters and language in general are God-given tools to bring the essential link of our souls to God's very essence into our consciousness.

4. In Kabbalah, there are two terms for "surrounding [light]": *sovev* and *makif*. The latter is related to *tokef* ("power" or "omnipotence"). In Hassidic teachings, it is explained that this is

the power of will, of which it is said, "there is nothing as strong as will" (see *Zohar* 2:162b; *Kuntres HaChinuch VehaHadrachah*, chapter 16). God's will to create is, in fact, His transcendent, all-encompassing light. "Transcendence" thus should not be misunderstood to mean "dissociated" from reality, but rather, "transcendence" is the Divine power by which God rules and changes nature as He wills. And so, the unique Name of God, the Name *Havayah*, is generally understood to refer to His supernatural power manifested as miracles, as those of the Exodus.

5. *Shemot Rabbah* 1:3.

6. This commandment thus implies that "they [the Jewish people] are My servants, and not servants to servants" (see *Bava Metzia* 10a).

7. *Avot* 3:6.

8. See *Shemot Rabbah* 4:2; *Zohar* 1:253a; *Sha'ar HaPesukim*, *Vayechi*; *Torah Or*, beginning of *Mishpatim*.

9. In the terminology of Hassidism: "the Egypt of holiness."

10. The commandment to appoint a king appears in Deuteronomy 17:15, which reads, "place, you shall place above yourself a king." The apparent redundancy of "place, you shall place" is interpreted in the *Zohar* (3:275b) to mean: "'place' above; 'you shall place' below." First, we must place God above ourselves as our one and only King; then, then, we may place upon ourselves a human king who will manifest God's kingdom on earth in full.

11. The first "king" of Israel—who can be seen as a prototype for all those who followed, since "all follows the beginning" (*Eiruvin* 41a)—was Moses himself, of whom it is said, "And there was a king in Jeshurun" (Deuteronomy 33:5).

Indeed, there are two opinions among the sages as to whom "a king in Jeshurun" refers (Deuteronomy 33:5). According to one opinion it refers to God, according to the other opinion it refers to Moses. Of the two major classical commentaries of the Torah, Rashi says that the king refers to God, whereas Ibn Ezra says that it refers to Moses. In accordance with the principle that "[both]

these and those are the words of the Living God" (*Eiruvin* 13b),
this verse itself may be seen to reflect the dependency of the lower
king (Moses) on the higher King (God), as the *Zohar* (3:275b, in
Raya Mehemna) interprets the verse "place, you shall place above
yourself a king" (see *Malchut Yisrael,* vol. 2, pp. 145 ff). Moreover,
in the case of Moses (and his successor in each generation), the
higher King and the lower king are manifest as one. (Moses'
kingship is "transparent," just as was the nature of his prophecy
[Numbers 12:8].)

The numerical value of the phrase "And there was a king in
Jeshurun" (*vayehi bishurun melech*) is 689, the value of *Netzach Yisrael,*
"the Eternity of Israel" (1 Samuel 15:29), a connotation both of
God, the supreme King, and the kingdom of Israel (the kingdom
of David) below. Note that 689 = 13 times 53. The phrase, "And
there was a king in Jeshurun," possesses 13 letters. Thus, the
average value of each of its letters is 53, the number of portions in
the Five Books of Moses, of whom it is said, in the previous verse
of the Torah, "Moses commanded us the Torah, an inheritance for
the congregation of Jacob" (Deuteronomy 33:4). This is the very
first verse that a father is instructed to teach his son, just as the
constant commandment related to it, corresponding to Moses and
to *netzach*, is the first of the constant commandments of the Torah.

12. Indeed, "all Jews are kings" (*Zohar* 2:26b; *Tikunei Zohar,*
introduction [1b]). A king is defined as "one who has no other
above him beside GOD, his God" (*Horayot* 3:3).

13. Psalms 84:8; *Berachot* 64a.

14. *Shabbat* 133b, *Y. Peah* 1, *Sotah* 14a, *Tana d'vei Eliahu Rabbah*
26. As we shall see, the first of the six constant commandments of
the Torah, belief in God's existence, is referred to as "faith in
general," while the third, belief in God's unity, is referred to as
"faith in particular." The same relationship applies with regard to
emulating God's ways implied in these commandments.

Implied in the first commandment is the aspiration of the soul
to emulate God in general (without emphasis on any one of His

attributes in particular: here the emphasis is "just as *He* is…").
Implied in the third is the aspiration of the soul to emulate, in
particular, the Divine attribute of mercy—"just as He is *merciful*,
so shall you be *merciful*."

The consciousness of the first commandment is of ascending
upwards, "I will be like the Most High" (Isaiah 14:14) in the sense
of: "I will become like God, the Most High, by emulating *Him*."
The consciousness of the third commandment is of progressing
forward; here, one is ever desirous to improve oneself and come
closer to God by emulating *His ways*.

In a certain sense, the desire to emulate *Him* is the desire to
emulate His omnipotence. (This, when rooted in arrogance, can
border on the heresy of the desire to be God, as is the meaning of
the verse "I will be like the most High" in its textual context.) The
desire to emulate (by the grace of God and in total subservience to
Him) God's omnipotence is the epitome of the experience of the
Exodus, the liberation of the soul from all confinements (just as
He is unbounded, and thereby all-powerful, so does the Jewish
soul, in consummate humility, strive to break out of all its
existential bounds).

In contrast, the consciousness of the third constant
commandment, to unify God, first implies unifying His indefinable
essence with His known attributes. To know this unity, we must
ourselves adopt His attributes—"just as He is merciful…."

15. *Tanya*, ch. 2., par. Job 31:2. In Job, the idiom reads "a part
[or 'portion'] of God from above." Numerically, "a part of God"
(*cheilek Elokah*) equals 180, the identical value of "from above"
(*mima'al*). 180 is also the numerical value of the word for "face"
(*panim*). Thus, the idiom "a part of God from above" alludes to the
Torah's description of God's revelation to Moses, "face to face"
(*panim el panim*, [Deuteronomy 33:10]), as well as to the way God
spoke and revealed the Torah to the entire Jewish people at Mt.
Sinai, "face to face" (*panim befanim*, [*ibid.* 5:4]).

To "face" someone is to make a full turn of 180 degrees (to turn from one's initial state of egocentricity to face another; the measurement of degrees is indeed a Torah measure). "Face to face" thus implies a complete cycle of 360 degrees, a revelation from above of God's infinite light that "surrounds all worlds" (*sovev kol almin*).

Chapter Four

1. Exodus 20:3.

2. At Mt. Sinai, the entire Jewish people heard the first two commandments directly from the mouth of God (*Makot* 24a). In the Torah, the first two of the Ten Commandments appear in the same paragraph (*parashah*), whereas each of the remaining eight of the Ten Commandments appears in a separate paragraph.

3. This includes spiritual forces present in nature, such as those manipulated by the human psyche through witchcraft, divination, spirits, superstitions, etc.

In the verse "And you shall know this day and take to heart that GOD is God in the heavens above and on the earth below; there is no other" (Deuteronomy 4:39), the spiritual forces present in nature are referred to, relatively, as "the heavens above," in contrast to the overtly natural forces, which are referred to as "the earth below." "There is no other" parallels our commandment: "You shall have no other gods before Me."

4. This reliance is known as "worshipping idols in purity." See *Avodah Zarah* 8a. See *VaYadata Moscow*, p. 18; *Likutei Sichot*, vol. 1, p. 190.

5. *Zohar* 1:36a.

6. See *Nidah* 31a.

7. The numerical value of the first word of the Fifth Commandment, "Honor [your father and your mother]" is 26, the value of God's essential Name, *Havayah*. This teaches us that in honoring our parents we are honoring God, for He has chosen our parents to be partners with Him in creating us.

8. As explained earlier, the seemingly supernatural forces of nature are referred to as "heavens above" in contrast to the overtly natural forces, "the earth below." But, in general, all created forces of nature are "earthly" in contrast to Divine reality, the "heavens"

from which God reveals Himself to Israel—particularly in the giving of the Torah, when God "spoke to you from heaven" (Exodus 20:19).

Here, the Torah refers to itself as being "from heaven." In fact, the idiom "from heaven" appears ten times in the Five Books of Moses, alluding to the Ten Commandments. The only other time it appears in Exodus (16:4) is in reference to the *manna* (the miraculous "bread from heaven" that our forefathers ate during the forty years of their sojourn in the desert from Egypt to the Promised Land); and the sages state that the Torah is allegorically connoted "bread from heaven" and indeed, "was only given to those who ate of the manna" (*Tanchuma, Beshalach* 20).

Thus, after quoting the verse from the Book of Deuteronomy (4:39), "And you shall know this day and take to heart that GOD is God in the heavens above and on the earth below; there is no other," Rabbi Shneur Zalman of Liadi (at the beginning of *Sha'ar HaYichud VehaEmunah*, p. 76b) focuses his discussion of the prohibition of idolatry exclusively on the dimension *below*, and even paraphrases the entire phrase "in the heavens above and on the earth below" simply as "the water *under* the earth"!

On the fifth day, the day corresponding to the *sefirah* of *hod*, the direction of *below*, God created the fish and the birds. Of all the days of creation, this is clearly the day that relates to *below*, the seas. The fish were the first to be created, after which God created the birds, which, according to the sages, were created from the swamps of the seas. The Torah makes a point of relating in particular the creation of the great sea creatures, the classic symbol of life below. Here, we see explicitly how the general direction of *below* contains its own relative *above* and *below*: the birds fly in the sky *above* while the fish swim in the waters *below*.

9. This can be seen in the Hebrew word for "nature" (*teva*); when used as a verb, it means "to drown," "to be submerged," as is said of the Egyptians in the Song of the Sea, "they drowned in the Red Sea" (Exodus 15:4). The Ten Commandments were given

to us when we were redeemed from the forces that governed Egypt.

10. The injunction to be whole and complete with God is explicitly stated in the Torah in the verse: "Be whole with GOD your God" (Deuteronomy 18:13). Although one could consider this a separate commandment, according to Maimonides it is not counted as one of the 613; he considers it a "general commandment," as he explains in his introduction to *Sefer HaMitzvot*. In contrast, Nachmanides does consider this verse an independent commandment, which he defines as belief in Divine Providence.

11. Psalms 15:2.

12. *Ibid* 119:1.

13. *Sefer Yetzirah* 5:7.

Chapter Five

1. Deuteronomy 6:4. This verse is composed of 25 letters; 25
= 5^2. In the *Zohar*, this commandment is referred to as "the higher
unification." Following this declaration of faith, we immediately
add the statement: "Blessed be the Name of His glorious kingdom
forever and ever," which is referred to in the *Zohar* as "the lower
unification" (see *Sha'ar HaYichud VehaEmunah*, at length). This
statement is composed of 24 letters; when added to the first verse,
$25 \perp 24 = 49 = 7^2$. This alludes to the consummate rectification of
all the 6 directions of Divine space around us together with
ourselves within, each of the 7 reflecting all the 7 (as in the 49 days
of the Counting of the *Omer*—7 weeks each of 7 days); "the lower
unification" thus serves to connect "the higher unification," the
front of our Divine consciousness, to all its other directions as well
as to the consciousness of ourselves within.

See Supplementary Essay, #27, "Three Pairs," p. 201.

2. In Hebrew, "to hear" also means "to understand."

3. Deuteronomy 4:35.

4. These two states of faith in God are alluded to in the verse:
"The *tzadik* shall live by his faith" (Habakkuk 2:4). The word for
"by his faith" (*be'emunato*) permutes to spell "two levels of faith"
(*beit emunot*): "faith in general" ("I am GOD, your God…") and
"faith in particular" ("Hear, O Israel…"). Also see at length,
Derech Mitzvotecha 44b ff.

5. The *Zohar* (3:103a, *inter alia*) refers to "faith in general"
metaphorically as "the shadow of faith," from the verse in Psalms
(121:5), "GOD is your shadow at your right hand." Here, we find
the directions *above* ("your shadow") and *right* ("your right hand")
juxtaposed.

We are taught in Hassidism that just as the first of the Ten
Commandments (*above*) includes, in particular, all the 248 positive

commandments of the Torah (see *Tanya*, ch. 20 [25b]), so does the commandment to love God (*right*) include (i.e., motivate us to perform) all the 248 positive commandments (*ibid.*, ch. 4 [8a]).

In truth, every two (or more) of the six directions of our meditation interrelate in some specific sense, thereby reinforcing one another in our consciousness. We will meet several additional examples of this in the course of our meditation. The more we integrate the meditation of "Living in Divine Space," the more we discover new interrelationships, whether based on direct experience or derived from Torah texts.

6. See Supplementary Essay #14, "Unity," p. 152.

7. See *Tanya, Igeret HaKodesh* 11.

8. *Zohar* 1:27b, 3:179a; *Zohar Chadash* 21a; *Tikunei Zohar* #56; *Mishneh Torah, Deiot* 2:3; Maimonides' commentary to *Avot* 2:10; cf. *Shabbat* 105b; *Nedarim* 22b; *Tanya, Igeret HaKodesh* 25.

9. Proverbs 3:17.

10. See Supplementary Essay #15, "Frontal Consciousness," p. 154.

11. *Shemot Rabbah* 3:6, etc.

12. The numerical value of the verse "Hear, O Israel, GOD is our God, GOD is one," 1118, is the lowest common multiple of the two Divine Names, the Name *Havayah* (26; 1118 = 26 times 43) and the Name *Elokim* (86; 1118 = 86 times 13), alluding to their absolute unity, here manifest.

13. *Tanya*, ch. 2.

14. Isaiah 65:22.

15. Ezekiel 17:6.

16. Zachariah 6:12.

17. Cf. *Tanya*, ch. 32 and ch. 45. This is not meant, of course, to exclude feeling mercy on oneself, on the Godly sparks that are in a state of spiritual exile in one's own body.

18. See Supplementary Essay #16, "Emulating Divine Mercy," p. 160.

Chapter Six

1. Deuteronomy 6:5. See Supplementary Essay #27, "Three Pairs," p. 201.

2. *Tanya*, ch. 4 (8a).

3. The numerical value of the Hebrew word *echad* ("one") is the same as that of the word *ahavah* ("love"), that is, 13. A further allusion to love in the verse "Hear, O Israel..." is that the root "hear" in Hebrew means, as well, "to gather [people or souls together]." Thus, "Hear, O Israel" is interpreted in Hassidic thought as "Gather, [in your mind and heart, all souls of] Israel [in perfect love for each and every soul; only thereafter will you merit to reveal in your soul God's absolute unity (beginning from His unity with the collective soul of Israel):] GOD is our God, GOD is one. [From this,] you will [come to consummate] love [of] God Himself, with all your heart, and with all your soul, and with all your might."

4. *Shenei HaMeorot* 2:2, quoted in *Magid Devarav LeYaakov, addendum* 12 (ed. *Kehot*), etc. See *Sifrei, VeEtchanan* 8.

5. The innate connection between these two commandments is alluded to by the fact that the words for "love" (*ahavah*) and "one" (*echad*) have the same numerical value (13), as noted above. Indeed, there are 13 unique manifestations of love: the love of God for Israel and the love of Israel for God; the love of teacher for pupil, of pupil for teacher and between pupils; the love of husband to wife and of wife to husband and between fellow-Jews; the love of parents to children and of children to parents and between siblings; the love of king to subjects and of subjects to their king. (These are the 13 manifestations of the *one* essential attribute of *love*, as we have explained at length earlier.) Furthermore, *ahavah* and *echad* equal together (2 times 13) the numerical value of God's essential Name, *Havayah* (26). This

indicates that by our fulfilling the two commandments of knowing God's unity and loving Him, God becomes the total reality of our lives.

6. As in the rabbinic injunction: "The left [hand] pushes away and the right [hand] draws close" (*Sotah* 47a; *Ruth Rabbah* 2:16; *Zohar* 3:187b). And so, in the Song of Songs (2:6, 8:3), we find: "His left hand is under my head, and His right hand embraces me."

"His left hand is under my head" is interpreted in Hassidic teachings to mean that His left hand supports our sense of self-consciousness, our experience of self as both independent and lowly. We shall see in the following chapter that the rectified consciousness of *left*, fear, produces both a sense of "removed" independence as well as lowliness. This is the meaning of "the left [hand] pushes away." Here is a case of fear preceding and resulting in love, the most common order of the manifestation of these emotions in the soul, as explained in *Tanya* (ch. 41 and 43).

7. *Shabbat* 21a.

8. *Tanya*, ch. 44.

9. *Berachot* 9:5.

10. As explained earlier, this recognition is implicit in the commandment to unify God—"Hear, O Israel, GOD [the merciful One] is our God [our life-force], GOD [the merciful One] is one."

Chapter Seven

1. Deuteronomy 10:12. This is the opening verse of the passage in the Torah known as "the passage of fear." See Supplementary Essay #17, "Fear," p. 163.

2. True awe of God, "shamefaced fear," is the third level of fear that will be explained.

3. *Tanya*, ch. 4 (8a).

4. This is referred to in Kabbalah and Hassidism as times of "constricted consciousness" (*katnut mochin*).

5. Rabbi Hillel of Paritch, beginning of *Chinuch Katan* (printed as an appendix to vol. 1 of his *Pelach HaRimon*).

6. We have previously identified "transcending limitations" with the Exodus from Egypt, the *above*-consciousness of our meditation. Here, then, we identify an inter-relationship between *above* and *left*. Conscious of the Divine *above*, we transcend the limitations of our spiritual bondage to any power other than He. Conscious of the Divine *left*, we transcend our previous level of love for God, never satisfied with our present, existentially limited level of Divine service, ever breaking through to new horizons of love for God.

7. In particular, the elevated evil inclination ignites the spark of "love as fire," whereas fear of God ever fans its ardent flame.

8. *Tanya*, ch. 40 (p. 55a), quoting *Sha'ar HaYichudim* 11. See Supplementary Essay #18, "The Inverted Seal," p. 168.

9. *Tikunei Zohar* 80a.

10. *Sanhedrin* 74a. This is based on the phrase, "and live in them" (Leviticus 18:5), which the sages interpret to mean, "and not die by them."

11. par. Ecclesiastes 5:1.

12. For which reason we are taught that the *sefirah* of *malchut* ("kingdom"), whose inner experience is *shiflut* ("lowliness"), is

"built" by the power of *gevurah* ("might"), whose inner experience
is fear.

Chapter Eight

1. Numbers 15:39. Note that the sources in the Torah for all of the first five constant commandments appear in their normal order, from the beginning of the Torah to its end. Only here do we "backtrack" in the order of the Torah (as did the sages in compiling the three paragraphs of the *Shema*). This is seemingly appropriate for the consciousness of the *back*!

To understand this phenomenon in greater depth, we must remember that *back* in Kabbalah and Hassidism is generally interpreted to imply "forgetting." One is not aware or conscious of that which is behind one, and thus, the *back* implies repression into the subconscious. The Torah states that forgetfulness is a result of the arrogance of the heart ("and your heart shall be haughty [literally: 'become uplifted'] and you shall forget" [Deuteronomy 8:14]). Arrogant people face only themselves; all else is repressed and forgotten.

By fear, we nullify or neutralize the haughtiness of the heart, as explained earlier, and so become able to remember that which we have forgotten due to our haughtiness. Thus, after fear, we "remember" to backtrack in the order of the Torah just as the farmer returns during the harvest to find forgotten sheaves. This very commandment begins with negating thoughts of arrogance, as will be explained.

See Supplementary Essay #27, "Three Pairs," p. 201.

2. The sages interpret that "after your heart" refers to heretical thoughts (*minut*) and "after your eyes" refers to licentious thoughts (*zenut*) (*Sifri, Bamidbar* 115, s.v. *v'lo taturu*). In the soul, heretical thoughts derive from arrogance, as the sages teach, "He and I cannot dwell under the same roof" (*Sotah* 5a). Licentious thoughts derive from lust.

This, the last of the six constant commandments of the Torah, corresponds to the *sefirah* of *yesod* ("foundation"), which, in the body, corresponds to the procreative organ, the seat of sexual desire. And so, the continuation of the verse, "and you shall not stray after your heart and after your eyes *after* which you go astray [*zonim*, from the word *zenut*, 'licentiousness']," indicates that the general guard of our consciousness, our spiritual *back*, relates to *zenut*. (The simple meaning of the text—"after your heart and after your eyes"—is that we first conjure lustful images in our hearts, whether consciously or unconsciously, and then look for them with our eyes.)

While the primary evil of our *back* (subconscious) relates to lust, the primary evil of our *front* (conscious) relates to arrogance. Our subconscious lust first manifests itself in the consciousness as thoughts of heresy and then continues to become overt thoughts of *zenut*.

3. See Supplementary Essay #19, "Being on Guard" (p. 173).

4. Cf. *Shabbat* 55a; *Sanhedrin* 1:1; *Bereishit Rabbah* 81:2; *Devarim Rabbah* 1:7; *Zohar* 1:2b.

5. Proverbs 10:25.

6. *Berachot* 61a.

7. See Supplementary Essay #20, "An Allusion to the Six Constant Commandments" (p. 176).

8. The word "stray" (*taturu*) in this verse also means "search out" or "explore," as in "to explore (*latur*) the land" (Numbers 13:16, 14:36, etc.). Indeed, the verse "and you shall not stray..." appears at the end, the *back*, of the Torah-portion (*Shelach*) that begins with the story of the spies who were sent "to explore the land."

The word *taturu* is also related to the word *Torah*, derived from the verb "to instruct." Thus, "and you shall not stray" implies not searching for foreign spiritual paths, for would-be "torahs." The sages teach us: "[if someone says that] there is wisdom amongst the nations, believe it, [but if he says that] there is Torah amongst the nations, do not believe it" (*Eichah Rabbah* 2:13).

9. As did Amalek (see Deuteronomy 25:18), the arch-enemy of Israel. In particular, the sages teach that Amalek blemished Israel's holy covenant identified with the procreative organ [*Bamidbar Rabbah* 13:3], corresponding to this last of the six constant commandments of the Torah. Above, we saw that remembrance of Amalek corresponds to this constant commandment. Based on the words of the prophet Obadiah (1:18), we learn that Amalek will be vanquished by the seed of Joseph, the archetypal soul that corresponds to the *sefirah* of *yesod*, he who stood the trial of guarding his holy covenant, when Potiphar's wife sought to seduce him.

10. During the era of the First Temple, certain elements of the populace fell into idolatrous practices. In the Mishnah (*Sukah* 5:4) it is stated that, as part of the ceremonies in the second Temple on the festival of *Sukot*, the people exclaimed, "Our fathers, when they were in this place, had their backs to the Temple, and their faces eastward, and they bowed down eastward to the sun. But as for us, we are for God and our eyes are directed to God!" We see here that in the Mishnaic idiom, that which is undesired is associated with the back. When we reach the level of consciousness that "we are for God and our eyes are directed to God" (as in the verse, "I place GOD in front of me always," discussed above), then we may know that the foreign enticements of this world are truly behind us.

11. This sin is known as "the blemishing of the covenant" (*pegam habrit*), i.e., the wasteful spilling of one's vital, procreative seed, either literally or allegorically, in the sense of the wasteful squandering of one's God-given energy and talents.

The numerical value of *pegam habrit*, 740, is the same as that of "an actual part of God from on high" (*cheilek Elokah mima'al mamash*), the phrase that best depicts the essence of the Divine soul of Israel. From this we understand that, more than any other transgression, *pegam habrit* blemishes, i.e., conceals or represses, the consciousness of the true and essential source of one's soul in Divinity.

740 is also the numerical value of *Ribono shel Olam*, "Master of the Universe," a common appellation of God, the omnipotent Creator and King of the universe. The essence of the Divine soul of Israel is indeed an actual part of the Master of the Universe, and when our "covenant" (*brit*) is pure, when we have done *teshuvah* and rectified our *pegam habrit*, we are able to manifest our essential connection to the Master of the Universe, for "the *tzadik* [the 'righteous one,' whose *brit* is pure] decrees and God fulfills; God decrees and the *tzadik* nullifies" (see *Shabbat* 59b, quoting Job 22:28).

12. *Bava Batra* 25a.

13. Cf. *Zohar* 3:243a.

Chapter Nine

1. Psalms 109:4.

2. See Supplementary Essay #21, "All Sevenths are Beloved," p. 178.

3. This opinion (based on *Berachot* 21a and *Sukah* 38a) is quoted by Nachmanides in his *Hasagot* to Maimonides' *Sefer HaMitzvot*, Positive Commandment #5. In *Magen Avraham* to *Shulchan Aruch, Orach Chaim* 106:2, it is stated that this is in fact the majority opinion.

4. Cf. the conclusion of Nachmanides' commentary *ad loc.* In *Magen Avraham, loc. cit.*, this opinion is cited in the name of *Sefer Mitzvot Katan*.

5. Maimonides (*Mishneh Torah, Tefilah* 1:1-2); he states, however, that the Written Torah does not prescribe specific times or liturgy for prayer. On the entire subject, cf. *Sefer HaChinuch* 433 and *Derech Mitzvotecha* 115a.

6. *Megilah* 17b, *Berachot* 33a, *Tur* and *Shulchan Aruch, Orach Chaim* 81 and 106. Of course, a woman is permitted to pray the complete three prayers a day if she so desires. See Supplementary Essay #22, "Evening, Morning, and Noon," p. 183.

7. *Berachot* 21a; *Pesachim* 44b; *Y. Shabbat* 1:2. Nachmanides (*ibid.*) also notes the conceptualization of prayer as an ideal state of consciousness in one's general service of God.

8. See Supplementary Essay #23, "The Limit Process," p. 188.

9. *Berachot* 26b.

10. See Supplementary Essay #24, "The Miracle of Prayer" (p. 192).

11. The numerical value of the letter *vav*, which means "and," is 6. Thus, the above-quoted verse, "And I am prayer" (*Va'ani tefilah*) can also be read, "[There are] six [constant commandments

defining the six directions of Divine space, with the seventh,] I-am-prayer, [within them]."

12. *Midrash Tanchuma, Naso* 7:1.

13. These three levels (super-rational faith, mind, and physical world) can be seen as corresponding to the three eras into which the sages divide the 6,000 years of history: 2,000 years of chaos, 2,000 years of Torah, and 2,000 years centering on the Messiah (*Sanhedrin* 97a; *Avodah Zarah* 9a; *Tana d'vei Eliahu Rabbah* 2).

Chaos alludes to the unordered infinite vastness of the unconscious mind. The intellect is the tool used to fathom the Torah (*Zohar* 2:85a, etc.), and the Messianic era is the time at which Divine consciousness will pervade all aspects of reality, as stated above. Prayer is the "weapon" or "tool" of the Messiah (see *Likutei Moharan* 2), expressing the faith of the Jewish soul in his imminent arrival. For this reason, the Arizal states that in these last two millennia, the central rectification of reality is accomplished by means of prayer, rather than Torah study, as was the case prior to this (*Pri Eitz Chaim, Sha'ar HaTefilah* 7; *Tanya, Kuntres Acharon* 4 [155a] and 8 [162a]).

14. This is in fact the order in which Maimonides presents these commandments in his *Mishneh Torah*. The sixth commandment relates to the rectification of one's character and deeds—"you shall not stray after your heart and after your eyes...in order that you remember and perform all My commandments...."—in contrast to the first five, which define the parameters of our relationship with God. He therefore places the first five in "The Laws of the Fundaments of the Torah" and the sixth later, in "The Laws of Attitudes."

Clearly, the first two positive commandments, according to the enumeration of Maimonides, the belief in God's existence (and Providence) and the belief in His absolute unity, are the most fundamental. As explained earlier, the former (the *above* direction) is how we relate to the world in general ("overall"), whereas the latter (the forward direction) is how we relate to the world in detail.

Chapter Ten

1. This, of course, does not exclude meditating any time of day that one has the proper peace of mind.

2. See *HaYom Yom*, 20 *Tamuz*, and *Klal Gadol BaTorah*, p. 17 ff.

3. Zachariah 2:8-9.

4. *Pesikta Rabati, Shabbat v'Rosh Chodesh* 3.

5. *Berachot* 51a.

6. Genesis 28:14.

7. *Kelim* 1:6.

8. See Supplementary Essay #25, "Ritual Baths, the Land of Israel, and the Sukah," p. 194.

9. Numbers 34:52, *et al.* We are taught that "the atmosphere of the Land of Israel makes one wise" (*Bava Batra* 158b). Even the wisest of Jews, when entering the Promised Land, will tend to change their mind with regard to previous assumptions and opinions (*Rashbam ad loc.*). Entering the atmosphere of the Land of Israel is entering Divine space, a space encompassing us from all sides, a space conducive to Divine inspiration.

The command to purify the Land of Israel from all idolatry is interpreted to mean that in the Holy Land we must search for the most concealed traces of idolatry and uproot them from even subterranean locations (*Avodah Zarah* 45b), from *below*. The holy atmosphere of the Land of Israel is conducive to enlightening us to recognize even the subtlest nuances of mistaken thinking in order to uproot them. These mistaken ways of thinking are the subtlest forms of spiritual idolatry, all stemming from conscious or unconscious reliance on natural causation, the mindspace of the Diaspora.

10. Genesis 14:18.

11. *Ibid.* 22:14. Literally, the phrase reads "GOD shall see," but "shall see" (*yireh*) is spelled the same way as "fear/awe" (*yirah*).

12. *Shemot Rabbah* 15:8.

13. *Pesachim* 88a.

14. Rashi interprets: "'GOD is our God'—in this world only we, the Jewish people, recognize GOD and serve Him; 'GOD is one'—but in the future, all peoples on earth will recognize Him, the God of Israel, and serve Him, as it is said: 'For then will I make the nations pure of speech, so that they will all call upon the Name of GOD, to serve Him together' [Zephaniah 3:9], and so it is written: 'And GOD will be King over the whole world; on that day, GOD will be one and His Name will be one' [Zachariah 14:9]."

All peoples will come to serve God in His Holy Temple in Jerusalem, as it is said, "My House shall be called a house of prayer for all peoples" (Isaiah 56:7). In the Temple, it will become revealed to all the nations on earth that "GOD is one." At that time, the words of Abraham—the "father of all nations" (Genesis 17:4-5)—referring to the Temple site will become fulfilled: "...GOD will see...GOD will be seen." Then will Isaiah's prophecy (52:8) also be fulfilled: "For eye to eye shall they see when GOD returns to Zion."

15. See Supplementary Essay #26, "Marital Union," p. 198.

Chapter Eleven

1. Exodus 33:21. From the very fact that in Hebrew the same word (*makom*) denotes both "place" and "space," we may infer that all space is indeed "place," i.e., a "location" for something to be situated. This implies, as taught in Kabbalah and Hassidism, that in truth, there is no empty space, no absolute vacuum; all created space is, and is no more than, a place for creation, and indeed, something is created in every point of space.

2. *Bereishit Rabbah* 68:10.

3. For example, we find in the Passover *Haggadah*: "Blessed be the Omnipresent One [literally, 'the Place']." Another appearance of "the Place" referring to God Himself is in the Talmud (*Avodah Zarah* 7b): "One should always recount God's [lit., 'the Place's'] praises first and then pray." Here we find an allusion to our meditation. By recounting God's praises, we create a Divine space around ourselves, in which we pray—"and I am prayer."

In Kabbalah, we are taught that when each of the four letters of the Name *Havayah* is squared, their sum equals 186, the numerical value of the Hebrew word for "place" (*makom*). This Kabbalistic "intention" (*kavanah*) of the word refers to God's transcendent light ("space" as Divine transcendence, as will be explained).

Alluding to God's immanent light ("space" as Divine immanence, as will be explained) is the intention that *Makom* (186) equals 6 times 31 (*Kel*), the Name of God associated with the *sefirah* of *chesed* in particular. This Name *Kel* also means "toward" (*el*), implying a vector force aimed at a specific direction. Thus, 6 times *Kel* alludes to the six directions of created, three-dimensional space, all infused with Divine power.

4. See beginning of *Eitz Chaim*.

5. The sages state, "Before the world was created, only the Holy One, blessed be He, and His great Name existed" (*Pirkei d'Rabbi Eliezer* 3). In Kabbalah, it is noted that the numerical values of "His Name" (*shemo*) and "will" (*ratzon*) are the same (346), indicating, as stated in the text, that the primordial Divine will to create the world is identical with God's Name that existed together with Him before the world's creation.

6. Deuteronomy 4:35.

7. These four levels of space, two "concealed" and two "revealed," correspond to the four letters of the Name *Havayah*, as follows:

	in reality	in Divine service
yud	God's very essence	"there is nothing other than Him"
hei	His transcendent light; His will to create	the union of the created in the Creator in love
vav	the "ray" of Divine creative energy; His immanent light	relationship and sincere concern of one (God) for the other (man)
hei	the apparent vacuum or "womb" of creation	"separation"; existential longing for God

Glossary

Note: all foreign terms are Hebrew unless otherwise indicated. Terms preceded by an asterisk have their own entries.

Abba (אבא, "father" [Aramaic]): the *partzuf* of *chochmah.

Adam Kadmon (אדם קדמון, "primordial man"): the first *world.

Arich Anpin (אריך אנפין, "the long face" or "the infinitely patient one"): the external *partzuf* of *keter (the inner dimension is *Atik Yomin*). In psychological terms, it is synonymous with will. It possesses its own *keter* (the *gulgalta*), and its own *chochmah (*mocha stima'ah*).

Asiyah (עשיה, "action"): the lowest of the four *worlds.

Atbash: (אתב״ש): the simple reflective transformation. The first letter of the alphabet is paired with the last, the second with the second-to-last, and so on. These letters of these pairs may then be interchanged.

א	ב	ג	ד	ה	ו	ז	ח	ט	י	כ
ת	ש	ר	ק	צ	פ	ע	ס	נ	מ	ל

Atik: short for *Atik Yomin.

Atik Yomin (עתיק יומין, "the ancient of days" [Aramaic]): the inner *partzuf* of *keter.

Atika Kadisha (עתיקא קדישא, "the holy ancient One" [Aramaic]): in some contexts, this term is a synonym for *Atik Yomin*; in others, for *keter in general.

Atzilut (אצילות, "Emanation"): First and highest of the four
*worlds emanating from *Adam Kadmon*.

Av (אב, "father"): the fifth month of the Jewish calendar.

Ba'al Shem Tov (בעל שם טוב, "Master of the Good Name [of
God]"): Title of Rabbi Yisrael ben Eliezer (1698-1760), founder
of the Chassidic movement (*Chassidut*).

Ba'al Teshuvah (בעל תשובה, "one who returns"): one who
returns to the ways of Judaism and adherence to Jewish law
after a period of estrangement. Often used in contrast to a
tzadik, who has not undergone such a period. The *ba'al teshuvah*
strives continually to ascend, return and become subsumed
within God's essence; the *tzadik* strives primarily to serve God
by doing good deeds and thus drawing His light into the world.
Ideally these two paths are meant to be inter-included, i.e. that
every Jew should embody both the service of the *ba'al teshuvah*
and that of the *tzadik*, as well. See also *teshuvah*.

Beriah (בריאה, "creation"): the second of the four *worlds.

Binah (בינה, "understanding"): the third of the ten *sefirot*.

Birur (ברור, "separation," "choosing," or "refinement"): a type of
tikun in which one must work to separate good from evil in
any given entity, and then reject the evil and accept the good.
This may be done actively or in one's consciousness. See *yichud*.

Bitachon (בטחון, "confidence"): 1. the feeling of confidence in
one's God-given power to take initiative and succeed in one's
mission in life. See *emunah*. 2. The inner experience of the
sefirah of *netzach*. 3. ("trust"): the feeling that God will
orchestrate events in accord with the greatest revealed good.
This passive *bitachon* is associated with the *sefirah* of *hod*.

Bitul (בטול, "annihilation"): any of a number of states of
selflessness or self-abnegation. The inner experience of the
sefirah of *chochmah*.

Chabad (חב״ד), acronym for **chochmah,* **binah,* **da'at* (חכמה בינה דעת, "wisdom, understanding, knowledge"): 1. the first triad of **sefirot,* which constitute the intellect (see *Chagat, Nehi*). 2. the branch of *Chassidut founded by Rabbi Shneur Zalman of Liadi (1745-1812), emphasizing the role of the intellect and meditation in the service of God.

Chagat (חג״ת), acronym for **chesed,* **gevurah,* *tiferet (חסד גבורה תפארת, "loving-kindness, strength, beauty"): the second triad of **sefirot,* which together constitute the primary emotions (see *Chabad, Nehi*).

Chasadim: plural of *chesed (second sense).

Chayah (חיה, "living one"): the second highest of the five levels of the *soul.

Chesed (חסד, "loving-kindness"; pl. חסדים, *chasadim*): 1. the fourth of the ten **sefirot.* 2. a manifestation of this attribute, specifically in **da'at.*

Chochmah (חכמה, "wisdom" or "insight"): the second of the ten **sefirot.*

Da'at (דעת, "knowledge"): 1. the unifying force within the ten **sefirot.* 2. the third *sefirah* of the intellect, counted as one of the ten *sefirot* when *keter*, the superconscious, is not counted.

Din (דין, "judgment"; pl. דינים, *dinim*): 1. a synonym for **gevurah.* 2. a manifestation of this attribute. 3. a synonym for **kal vechomer.*

Emunah (אמונה, "faith" or "belief"): 1. the belief that no matter what God does, it is all ultimately for the greatest good, even if it does not appear so to us presently. See **bitachon.* 2. the inner experience associated with **reisha d'lo ityada.*

Gedulah (גדלה, "greatness"): a synonym for **chesed.*

Gematria (גימטריא, "numerology" [Aramaic]): The technique of comparing Hebrew words and phrases based on their numerical values.

Gevurah (גבורה, "power" or "strength"; pl. גבורות, *gevurot*): 1. the fifth of the ten **sefirot*. 2. a manifestation of this attribute, specifically in **da'at*.

Gevurot: plural of **gevurah* (second sense).

Gulgalta (גלגלתא, "the skull" [Aramaic]): the **keter* of **Arich Anpin*. In psychological terms, the interface between pleasure and will, which serves as the origin of the super-conscious will.

Halachah (הלכה, "way" or "walking"): 1. the entire corpus of Jewish law. 2. a specific Jewish law.

Hassidism (חסידות, *Chassidut*, "piety" or "loving-kindness"): 1. An attribute or way of life that goes beyond the letter of the law. 2. The movement within Judaism founded by Rabbi Yisrael Ba'al Shem Tov (1648-1760), the purpose of which is to awaken the Jewish people to its own inner self through the inner dimension of the Torah and thus to prepare the way for the advent of **Mashiach*. 3. The oral and written teachings of this movement.

Havayah (יהו־ה), also known as the Tetragrammaton ("four-letter Name"). Due to its great sanctity, this Name may only be pronounced in the Holy Temple, and its correct pronunciation is not known today. When one is reciting a complete Scriptural verse or liturgy, it is read as if it were the Name *Adni*; otherwise one says *Hashem* (השם, "the Name") or *Havayah* (הויה, a permutation of the four letters of this Name).

Havayah is the most sacred of God's Names. Although no name can fully express God's essence, the Name *Havayah* in certain contexts *refers* to God's essence. In these cases it is called "the higher Name *Havayah*" and is termed "the essential Name" (שם העצם), "the unique Name" (שם המיחד), and "the explicit Name" (שם המפרש).

Otherwise, the Name Havayah refers to God as He manifests Himself through creation. In these cases it is called "the lower Name Havayah," and its four letters are seen to depict in their form the creative process and allude to the worlds, ten sefirot, etc., as follows:

		creation	worlds	*sefirot*
קוצו של י	upper "tip" of the *yud*	will to create	*Adam Kadmon*	*keter*
י	*yud*	contraction	*Atzilut*	*chochmah*
ה	*hei*	expansion	*Beriah*	*binah*
ו	*vav*	extension	*Yetzirah*	the six *midot*
ה	*hei*	expansion	*Asiyah*	*malchut*

The lower Name *Havayah* appears on several levels. It is first manifest as the light within all the *sefirot*. It thus possesses on this level ten iterations, which are indicated as ten vocalizations—each using one of the ten vowels. (These are only meditative "vocalizations," since it is forbidden to pronounce the Name *Havayah* with any vocalization, as we have said.) For example, when each of its four letters is vocalized with a *kamatz*, it signifies the light within the *sefirah* of *keter*; when they are each vocalized with a *patach*, it signifies the light within the *sefirah* of *chochmah*. The other Names of God (including the subsequent manifestations of the Name *Havayah*) refer to the vessels of the *sefirot*. In the world of *Atzilut*, where these Names are principally manifest, both the vessels and the lights of the *sefirot* are manifestations of Divinity.

The second manifestation of the lower Name *Havayah* is as the vessel of the *sefirah* of *chochmah*. (This is alluded to in the verse, "*Havayah* in *chochmah* founded the earth" [Proverbs 3:19].)

Its third manifestation is as the vessel of the *sefirah* of *binah*. This manifestation is indicated by the consonants of the Name vocalized with the vowels of (and read as) the Name *Elokim* (for example, Deuteronomy 3:24, etc.).

The most basic manifestation of the lower Name *Havayah* is in the *sefirah* of *tiferet*, whose inner experience is mercy. The Name *Havayah* in general is associated with "the principle of mercy," since mercy is the most basic emotion through which God relates .. His creation. In this, its most common sense, it is vocalized with the vowels of (and read as) the Name *Adnut*.

Hod (הוד, "splendor," "thanksgiving," "acknowledgment"): the eighth of the ten **sefirot*.

Ima (אמא, "mother" [Aramaic]): the **partzuf* of **binah*.

Kabbalah (קבלה, "receiving" or "tradition"): the esoteric dimension of the Torah.

Kabbalat Shabbat (קבלת שבת, "welcoming the Sabbath"): the series of psalms and hymns, etc. recited as a prelude to the Friday night prayer service, to mark the onset of the Sabbath.

Kav (קו, "line"): the ray of light beamed into the vacated space created in consequence of the **tzimtzum*.

Keter (כתר, "crown"): the first of the ten **sefirot*.

Lecha Dodi (לכה דודי, "Come, my beloved"): a hymn recited as part of **Kabbalat Shabbat*.

Lights: see *Sefirah*.

Lubavitch (ליובאוויטש, "City of Love" [Russian]): the town that served as the center of the **Chabad* movement from 1812 to 1915; the movement became known also after the name of this town.

Malchut (מלכות, "kingdom"): the last of the ten **sefirot*.

Mashiach (משיח, "anointed one," "messiah"): the prophesied descendant of King David who will reinstate the Torah-ordained monarchy (which he will head), rebuild the Holy **Temple*, and gather the exiled Jewish people to their homeland. This series of events (collectively called "the Redemption") will usher in an era of eternal, universal peace and true knowledge of God, called "the messianic era." There is also a prophesied messianic figure called *Mashiach ben* Joseph, who will rectify certain aspects of reality in preparation for the advent of *Mashiach ben* David.

Mazal (מזל, pl. מזלות, *mazalot*): 1. a spiritual conduit of Divine beneficence (from the root נזל, "to flow"). 2. specifically, the thirteen tufts of the "beard" of *Arich Anpin*. 3. a physical embodiment of such a spiritual conduit, such as a star, planet, constellation, etc. 4. specifically, the twelve constellations of the zodiac. 5. According to our sages, the Jewish people are not under the influence of the *mazalot* (*Shabbat* 156a). The Ba'al Shem Tov teaches that the Divine "nothingness" itself is the true *mazal* of the Jewish people.

Menorah (מנורה, "candelabrum"): the seven-branched candelabrum that was lit daily in the sanctuary of the *Tabernacle and, afterwards, in the Holy *Temple.

Midah (מדה, "measure" or "attribute," pl. מדות, *midot*): 1. an attribute of God. 2. specifically, one of the *sefirot* from *chesed* to *malchut*, in contrast to the higher *sefirot* of the intellect. 3. one of the thirteen attributes of mercy, which are part of the revelation of *keter.

Midot: plural of *midah.

Midrash (מדרש, "seeking"; pl. מדרשים, Midrashim): the second major body of the oral Torah (after the *Talmud), consisting of halachic or homiletic material couched as linguistic analyses of the Biblical text. An individual work of midrashic material is also called a Midrash, as is a specific analysis in midrashic style.

The Midrash is a corpus of many works written over the span of several centuries (roughly the second to the eighth CE), mostly in the Holy Land. The chief collection of homiletic midrashic material is the *Rabbah* ("great") series, covering the five books of Moses and the five scrolls. Other important collections are *Midrash Tanchuma*, *Midrash Tehilim*, *Pesikta d'Rav Kahana*, *Pirkei d'Rabbi Eliezer* and *Tana d'vei Eliahu*. Several later collections contain material that has reached us in its original form. These include *Midrash HaGadol* and *Yalkut Shimoni*. There are many smaller, minor Midrashim, as well; some of these are to be found in the collection *Otzar HaMidrashim*. Halachic Midrashim include the *Mechilta*, the *Sifra* and the *Sifrei*.

Mitzvah (מצוה, "commandment"; pl. מצות, *mitzvot*): one of the six hundred thirteen commandments given by God to the Jewish people, or seven commandments given by God to the nations of the world, at Mt. Sinai. 2. one of the seven commandments instituted by the sages. 3. idiomatically, any good deed.

Mitzvot: plural of *mitzvah*.

Mocha Stima'ah (מוחא סתימאה, "the hidden brain" [Aramaic]): the *chochmah* of *Arich Anpin*. In psychological terms, the power to generate new insight (כח המשכיל).

Mochin d'Abba (מוחין דאבא, "brains of *Abba*" [Aramaic]): a state of consciousness, mentality, or cognitive life force in which one experiences *chochmah*, or insight.

Mochin d'Ima (מוחין דאמא, "brains of *Ima*" [Aramaic]): a state of consciousness or mentality, or cognitive life force in which one experiences *binah*, or understanding or rationality.

Motzaei Shabbat (מוצאי שבת, "the outgoings of the Sabbath"): the night after the termination of *Shabbat; Saturday night.

Nefesh (נפש, "creature," "soul"): 1. the soul in general. 2. the lowest of the five levels of the *soul.

Nehi (נה"י), acronym for *netzach*, *hod*, *yesod* (נצח הוד יסוד, "victory, splendor, foundation"): the third triad of *sefirot*, which together constitute the attributes of behavior (see *Chabad*, *Chagat*).

Nekudim (נקדים, "dotted," "spotted"): the second stage in the development of the *world of *Atzilut.

Neshamah (נשמה, "soul"): 1. the soul in general. 2. the third of the five levels of the *soul.

Netzach (נצח, "victory," "eternity"): the seventh of the ten *sefirot.

Notrikun (נוטריקון, "acronym"): a method of interpretation in which a word is seen as comprising the initials or main consonantal letters of another word or phrase.

Nukvei d'Z'eir Anpin (נוקביה דזעיר אנפין [Aramaic]): the *partzuf of *malchut.

Omer: see *Sefirat HaOmer*.

Partzuf (פרצוף, "profile"; pl. פרצופים, *partzufim*): the third and final stage in the development of a *sefirah, in which it metamorphoses from a tenfold articulation of sub-*sefirot* into a human-like figure possessing the full set of intellectual and emotional powers. As such, it may thus interact with the other *partzufim* (which could not occur before this transformation. This stage of development constitutes the transition from *Tohu to *Tikun (or from *Nekudim* to *Berudim*, see under Worlds).

The *sefirot* develop into a primary and a secondary array of *partzufim*, as follows:

sefirah	primary *partzufim*		secondary *partzufim*	
keter	עתיק יומין *Atik Yomin*	"The Ancient of Days"	עתיק יומין *Atik Yomin*	[The male dimension of] "the Ancient of Days"
			נוקביה דעתיק יומין *Nukvei d'Atik Yomin*	[The female dimension of] "the Ancient of Days"
	אריך אנפין *Arich Anpin*	"The Long Face"	אריך אנפין *Arich Anpin*	[The male dimension of] "the Long Face"
			נוקביה דאריך אנפין *Nukvei d'Arich Anpin*	[The female dimension of] "the Long Face"
chochmah	אבא *Abba*	"Father"	אבא עילאה *Abba Ila'ah*	"Supernal Father"
			אמא עילאה *Ima Ila'ah*	"Supernal Mother"
binah	אמא *Ima*	"Mother"	ישראל סבא *Yisrael Saba*	"Israel the Elder"
			תבונה *Tevunah*	"Understanding"
the midot	זעיר אנפין *Z'eir Anpin*	"The Small Face"	ישראל *Yisrael*	"Israel"
			לאה *Leah*	"Leah"
malchut	נוקביה דזעיר אנפין *Nukvei d'Z'eir Anpin*	"The Female of *Z'eir Anpin*"	יעקב *Yaakov*	"Jacob"
			רחל *Rachel*	"Rachel"

Both of the secondary, male and female *partzufim* of *Atik Yomin* and *Arich Anpin* exist within the same figure. There are thus actually only ten distinct secondary *partzufim*.

Within any particular *partzuf*, the *sefirot* are arranged along three axes, right, left and middle, as follows:

left axis	center axis	right axis
	keter	
binah		*chochmah*
	da'at	
gevurah		*chesed*
	tiferet	
hod		*netzach*
	yesod	
	malchut	

In this arrangement, there are three triads of related *sefirot*: *chochmah-binah-da'at* (the intellect), *chesed-gevurah-tiferet* (the primary emotions) and *netzach-hod-yesod* (the behavioral attributes).

Pesach (פסח, "Passover"): the seven-day *yom tov* (eight days in the Diaspora) commemorating the liberation of the Jewish people from Egyptian slavery.

Rachamim (רחמים, "mercy"): the inner experience of the *sefirah* of *tiferet*.

Rasha (רשע, "wicked one," pl. רשעים, *resha'im*): one who succumbs to his urge to do evil and commits a sin. He retains this status until he does *teshuvah, at which point he becomes a *ba'al teshuvah*.

Reisha d'Arich (רישא דאריך, "the head of *Arich [Anpin]*" [Aramaic]): the lowest of the three "heads" of *keter*, synonymous with the *partzuf* of *Arich Anpin*. In psychological terms, super-conscious will.

Reisha d'Ayin (רישא דאין, "the head of nothingness" [Aramaic]): the middle of the three "heads" of *keter, related to the emotions of the *partzuf of *Atik Yomin. In psychological terms, super-conscious pleasure.

Reisha d'lo Ityada (רישא דלא אתידע [Aramaic]): the highest of the three "heads" of *keter, related to the *keter* and intellect of the *partzuf of *Atik Yomin. In psychological terms, super-conscious belief in God.

Rebbe (רבי, "my teacher"): 1. a term used to describe or address a teacher of Torah. 2. leader of a branch of the Chassidic movement.

Reshimu (רשימו, "residue," "impression"): the residual impression of the infinite Divine light that God withdrew from the vacated space resulting from the *tzimtzum.

Rosh Chodesh (ראש חדש, "new month"): the first day of a Jewish month, a day of celebration.

Rosh HaShanah (ראש השנה, "beginning of the year"): the Jewish New Year, commemorating the creation of man on the sixth day of creation, a day of universal judgment.

Ruach (רוח, "spirit"): a level of the *soul.

Sabbath: see Shabbat.

Sages: see *Torah.

Sefirah (ספירה, pl. ספירות, *sefirot*): a channel of Divine energy or life force. It is via the *sefirot* that God interacts with creation; they may thus be considered His "attributes."

There are altogether eleven *sefirot* spoken of in Kabbalistic literature. Inasmuch as two of them (*keter* and *da'at*) are two dimensions of a single force, the tradition generally speaks of only ten *sefirot*. Each *sefirah* also possesses an inner experience, as discussed in *Chassidut. The order of the *sefirot* is depicted in the chart on the following page.

Originally emanated as simple point-like forces, the *sefirot* at a certain stage develop into full spectrums of ten sub-*sefirot*. Subsequent to this, they metamorphose into **partzufim*.

Sefirot are composed of "lights" and "vessels." The light of any *sefirah* is the Divine flow within it; the vessel is the identity that flow takes in order to relate to or create some aspect of the world in a specific way. Inasmuch as all reality is created by means of the *sefirot*, they constitute the conceptual paradigm for understanding all reality.

name			inner experience	
keter	כתר	"crown"	1. אמונה 2. תענוג 3. רצון	1. "faith" 2. "pleasure" 3. "will"
chochmah	חכמה	"wisdom," "insight"	בטול	"selflessness"
binah	בינה	"understanding"	שמחה	"joy"
da'at	דעת	"knowledge"	יחוד	"union"
chesed	חסד	"loving-kindness"	אהבה	"love"
gevurah	גבורה	"strength," "might"	יראה	"fear"
tiferet	תפארת	"beauty"	רחמים	"mercy"
netzach	נצח	"victory," "eternity"	בטחון	"confidence"
hod	הוד	"splendor," "thanksgiving"	תמימות	"sincerity," "earnestness"
yesod	יסוד	"foundation"	אמת	"truth"
malchut	מלכות	"kingdom"	שפלות	"lowliness"

Sefirat HaOmer (ספירת העמר, "counting the *Omer*"): an *omer* is a dry measure mentioned in the Torah, and refers specifically to the measure of barley offered in the *Temple on the second day of *Pesach. Beginning with this day, the Jew is commanded to count the next forty-nine days, after which, on the fiftieth day, falls the holiday of *Shavuot.

Sefirot: plural of *sefirah.

Shabbat (שבת, "Sabbath"): the day of rest beginning sunset on Friday and ending at nightfall on Saturday.

Shacharit (שחרית, "morning"): the morning prayer service.

Shavuot (שבועות, "weeks"): the *yom tov* celebrating the wheat harvest and commemorating the giving of the Torah at Mt. Sinai.

Shechinah (שכינה, "indwelling"): the immanent Divine Presence that inheres within the universe, corresponding to the *sefirah* of *malchut*, the "feminine" aspect of Divinity.

Shema (שמע, "hear"): a compilation of three Biblical passages (Deuteronomy 6:4-9, 11:13-21, Numbers 15:37-41) beginning with this word, or sometimes, the first verse alone. The first verse is the fundamental profession of monotheism, "Hear O Israel, *God* is our God, *God* is one." We are commanded to recite the *Shema* twice daily, and it has been incorporated into the morning and evening services as well as the prayer said upon retiring at night. When reciting the first sentence, we are intended to consider ourselves ready to give up our lives rather than deny the oneness of God.

Shemini Atzeret (שמיני עצרת, "the eighth-day gathering"): the *yom tov* immediately following *Sukot, marking the end of the high-holiday season.

Soul: the animating life or consciousness within man (or any other creature, see *Sha'ar HaYichud VehaEmunah*, ch. 1). The Jew possesses an additional "Divine soul" which is focused on God's concerns in creation.

The essence of the soul possesses five manifestations ("names"), as follows:

name			experience
yechidah	יחידה	"unique one"	unity with God
chayah	חיה	"living being"	awareness of God as continually creating the world
neshamah	נשמה	"breath"	vitality of intelligence
ruach	רוח	"spirit"	vitality of emotion
nefesh	נפש	"creature"	physical vitality

Sukot (סכות, "huts," "booths"): the **yom tov* celebrating the ingathering of the harvest and commemorating the clouds of glory that accompanied the Jewish people on their desert trek after the exodus from Egypt.

Taharah (טהרה, ritual "purity"): the spiritual state in which one purified himself from a specific degree of **tumah* (or from *tumah* altogether), and is thus allowed to enter areas or touch, be touched by, or consume things or food he otherwise may not. In general, the process of attaining *taharah* involves some type of reaffirmation of life, such as immersion in a **mikveh*. The spiritual correlate to *taharah* is optimistic elation or joy in the service of God. See *tumah*.

Talmud: (תלמוד, "learning"): the written version of the greater part of the Oral **Torah, comprising mostly legal but also much homiletic and even some explicitly mystical material.

The Talmud comprises the *Mishnah* (משנה, "repetition") and the *Gemara* (גמרא, "completion"). The *Mishnah* is the basic compendium of the laws (each known as a *mishnah*) comprising the Oral Torah, redacted by Rabbi Yehudah the Prince in the second century CE. The *Mishnah* was elaborated upon over the next few centuries in the academies of the Holy Land and Babylonia; this material is the *Gemara*.

There are thus two Talmuds: the one composed in the Holy Land, known as the *Talmud Yerushalmi* ("The Jerusalem Talmud"), completed in the third century, and the one composed in Babylonia, known as the *Talmud Bavli* ("The Babylonian Talmud), completed in the sixth century.

The *Mishnah*—and *ipso facto* the Talmud—is divided into tractates. References to the *Mishnah* are simply the name of the tractate followed by the number of the chapter and individual *mishnah*. The Jerusalem Talmud was first printed in Venice, 1523-24. Although subsequent editions have generally followed the same pagination as this edition, it is nonetheless cited by chapter and *halachah* (i.e., individual *mishnah*) number, as is the *Mishnah*. References to it are therefore prefaced by "Y.," to distinguish them from references to the *Mishnah* itself. The Babylonian Talmud was first printed in its entirety in Venice, 1520-23, and subsequent editions have followed the same pagination as this edition. References to the tractates of the *Talmud Bavli* are simply by tractate name followed by page and column ("a" or "b").

Temimut (תמימות, "sincerity"): 1. earnestness and sincerity, either in one's conduct with his fellow man or in his connection to God. 2. The inner experience of **hod*.

Temple (or "Holy Temple"; Hebrew: בית המקדש, "house of the sanctuary"): The central sanctuary in Jerusalem which serves as the physical abode of the indwelling of God's Presence on earth and as the venue for the sacrificial service. The Temple is the focal point of one's spiritual consciousness. The first Temple was built by King Solomon (833 BCE) and destroyed by the Babylonians (423 BCE); the second Temple was built by Zerubabel (synonymous, according to some opinions, with

Nehemiah, 353 BCE), remodeled by Herod and destroyed by the Romans (68 CE); the third, eternal Temple will be built by *Mashiach*.

Teshuvah (תשובה, "return"): the return of the individual (or community), after a period of estrangement, to a state of oneness with and commitment to God and His Torah. See **Ba'al Teshuvah*.

Tevunah (תבונה, "comprehension"): the lower of the two secondary **partzufim* which develop from the *partzuf* of **Ima*, the higher one being *Ima Ila'ah* (אמא עלאה).

Tiferet (תפארת, "beauty"): the sixth of the ten **sefirot*.

Tishah b'Av (תשעה באב, "the ninth of **Av*"): fast day commemorating the destruction of the two Temples, which occurred on this day.

Tikun (תקון, "rectification," pl. תקונים, *tikunim*): 1. a state of perfection and order. 2. "The world of *Tikun*" is the **world that first manifests this state, which is synonymous with the world of *Atzilut* (and *Berudim*, see Worlds). 3. the spiritual process of liberating the fragments of Divine light trapped within the material realm, unconscious of God's presence, thereby restoring the world to its initially intended state of perfection. This is accomplished through the performance of **mitzvot*. 4. a remedy prescribed against the effects of committing a specific sin.

Tikunim: plural of **tikun* (fourth sense).

Tohu (תהו, "chaos"): 1. the primordial, unrectified state of creation. 2. "The world of *Tohu*" is the **world which manifests this state, synonymous with the initial, premature form of the world of **Atzilut*. It itself develops in two stages: a stable form (*Akudim*) followed by an unstable form (*Nekudim*, see Worlds). The world of *Tohu* is characterized by "great lights" entering

premature "vessels," resulting in the "breaking of the vessels" (
שבירת הכלים). See *Tikun.*

Torah (תורה, "teaching"): God's will and wisdom as
communicated to man. It pre-existed creation, and God used
the Torah as His blueprint in creating the world.

God certainly communicated the teachings of the Torah in
some form to Adam, who then transmitted them orally from
generation to generation. However, God "officially" gave the
Torah to mankind c. 1313 BCE (and during the ensuing 40
years) at Mt. Sinai through Moses. The Ten Commandments
were pronounced in the presence of the entire Jewish people.

God gave the Torah in two parts: the Written Torah and the
Oral Torah. The Written Torah originally consisted of the Five
Books of Moses (the "Pentateuch"), the other books being
added later (see Bible). The Oral Torah was communicated
together with the Five Books of Moses as an explanation of
the laws and lore included in it. This material was later written
down by the sages of the Oral Torah in the form of the
*Talmud, the *Midrash, and the *Zohar. (All references to "our
sages" in this book refer to the sages who transmitted the Oral
Torah as recorded in these works.)

Tumah (טמאה, ritual "impurity"): a spiritual state contracted by
someone or something under various circumstances and to
various degrees, in which he is prohibited from entering various
holy areas or touching, being touched by, or consuming various
holy objects or foods. In general, the sources of *tumah* are in
some way associated with death (or a missed chance for
potential life) and the purification process involves some type
of reaffirmation of life. The spiritual correlate to *tumah* is
depression or despair. See *taharah.*

Triangle: the sum of all integers from 1 to a specific number. For
example, the triangle of five (Δ5) is $1 \perp 2 \perp 3 \perp 4 \perp 5 = 15$.

Tzadik (צדיק, "righteous" person; pl. צדיקים, *tzadikim*): someone who has fully overcome the evil inclination of his animal soul (and converted its potential into good). See *beinoni, rasha*.

Tzadikim: plural of **tzadik*.

Tzimtzum (צמצום, "contraction"): the contraction and "removal" of God's infinite light in order to allow for creation of independent realities. The primordial *tzimtzum* produced the "vacated space" (חלל) devoid of direct awareness of God's presence. See *Kav* and *Reshimu*.

Vessels: see *sefirah*.

World (Hebrew: עולם): a spiritual level of creation, representing a rung on the continuum of consciousness or awareness of God. In general, there are four worlds: **Atzilut*, **Beriah*, **Yetzirah*, and **Asiyah*. In particular, however, these four worlds originate from a fifth, higher world, **Adam Kadmon*. All ten **sefirot* and twelve **partzufim* are manifest in each world; however, since there is a one-to-one correspondence between the worlds and the *sefirot*, a particular *sefirah* dominates in each world.

The world of *Atzilut* is fundamentally different from the three subsequent worlds in that in it there is no awareness of self *per se*, while the three lower worlds are progressive stages in the development of self-awareness.

The worlds correspond to the Name *Havayah* and the **sefirot* as follows:

the Name Havayah	World	dominant sefirah	level of consciousness
קוצו של י	אדם קדמון *Adam Kadmon* "Primordial Man"	*keter*	Divine will to create and plan of creation
י	אצילות *Atzilut* "Emanation"	*chochmah*	solely of God; no self-awareness
ה	בריאה *Beriah* "Creation"	*Binah*	potential existence; formless substance
ו	יצירה *Yetzirah* "Formation"	*midot*	general existence: archetypes, species
ה	עשיה *Asiyah* "Action"	*malchut*	particular existence; individual creatures

In particular, the world of *Atzilut* develops out of *Adam Kadmon* in three stages (the names of which are taken from Genesis 30:10):

world		developmental stage	description	
עקודים *Akudim*	"bound," "striped"	ten lights in one vessel	stable chaos	תהו *Tohu*
נקודים *Nekudim*	"dotted," "spotted"	ten lights in ten vessels, unstable	unstable chaos, collapse	
ברודים *Berudim*	"patterned," "speckled"	ten lights in ten inter-included vessels; stable	stable, mature rectification	תקון *Tikun*

Whenever unqualified reference is made to the world of *Atzilut*, its final, mature stage is meant. It should be noted as well that our physical universe is *below* and "enclothes" the final two *sefirot* (*yesod* and *malchut*) of the spiritual world of *Asiyah* referred to above.

Yechidah (יחידה, "single one"): the highest of the five levels of the *soul.

Yesod (יסוד, "foundation"): the ninth of the ten *sefirot*.

Yetzirah (יצירה, "formation"): one of the four *worlds.

Yisrael Saba (ישראל סבא, "Israel the Elder" [Aramaic]): the lower of the two secondary *partzufim* which develop from the *partzuf* of *Abba, the higher being *Abba Ila'ah* (אבא עלאה, "the higher *Abba*").

Yom Kippur (יום כפור, "Day of Atonement"): the holiest day of the Jewish year, marked by fasting and *teshuvah*, particularly through confession of sin.

Yom Tov (יום טוב, "good day" or "holiday"): a festive holiday on which, with certain exceptions, weekday work is prohibited just as on *Shabbat.

Z'eir Anpin (זעיר אנפין, "the small face" [Aramaic]): the *partzuf* of the *midot, corresponding to the emotive faculties of the soul. In general, the concept of "finitude" or "finite power" is identified with *Z'eir Anpin*.

Zohar (זהר, "Brilliance"): One of the basic texts of the oral *Torah and Kabbalah, recording the mystical teachings of Rabbi Shimon bar Yochai (2nd century). The Zoharic literature includes the *Zohar* proper, the *Tikunei Zohar*, and the *Zohar Chadash*. The *Zohar* was printed in 1558 in both Mantua and Cremona, but standard pagination follows the Mantua edition.

Index

commandment to learn,
142
commandments of, 19
finding God through, 4
giving of, 114
Name of God, 110
Tree of Life, 105
vs. other paths, 69
Torah study
vs. prayer, 155
Tree, 46
Tree of Knowledge, 47
Tree of Life, 47, 105
Trust, 32
Truth, 67
Tzadik, 68
Tzimtzum, 91

W

Walking, 39
Water, 53, 54, 60, 155, 182,
190
upper and lower, 108
Western Wall, 175
Wings, 60, 205
Women, 122
breasts, 155
womb, 162, 170, 182,
196
World to Come, 34, 53,
165
Worlds, 97, 205
Worlds, Souls, Divinity,
152

Y

Yom Kippur, 86